IDENTITY COLLAGES

j/j hastain

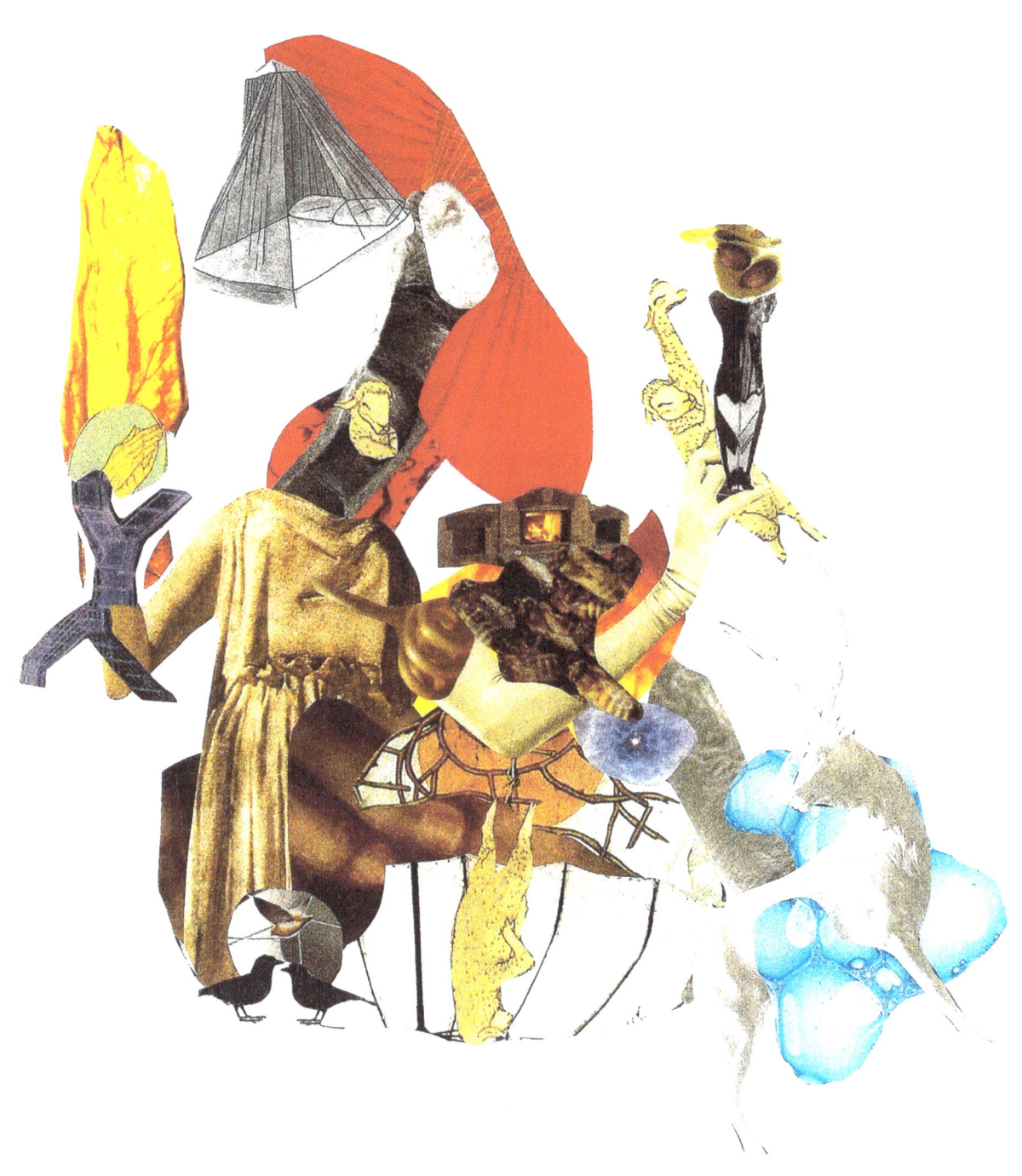

SPUYTEN DUYVIL
New York City

Acknowledgements:

Special thanks to the following journals where some of these collages
have been previously published (or are forthcoming): Gesture, Sein Und
Werden, Posit, Unlikely Books, Grey Book Press and Special Thanks to
Argos Books where some of these works appeared as *Forensics of the
Chamber*.

Library of Congress Cataloging-in-Publication Data

Hastain, J/J (Julia J.)
  Identity collages / j/j hastain.
    pages cm
  ISBN 978-0-923389-60-4
  1. Hastain, J/J (Julia J.)--Themes, motives. 2. Collage-
-United States. I. Title.
  N6537.H368A4 2014
  709.2--dc23
                              2014000167

IDENTITY COLLAGES

j/j hastain

What I call *Identity Collage* is both a materialization process and an embodiment state.

To begin each of these works I waited at a precipice: I slowed myself intentionally, tarried as a way of honoring what I was about to enter. There is materiality in the form which exists before the form that will be made; there are ways to dramatize upcoming linkage. Pause catalyzes future force.

What I was about to enter would end up revealing itself as a syrupy architecture, a site and state of queer plentitude, a form by which divergent forms *can* flourish.

My own experiences and memories are abject symmetries to me. They are dependent on *integration* in order that they live in *me* as part of an *always applicable poultice.* Whatever it is, I am constantly learning from both the thing itself and the way *I choose* to enter it.

It is my hope that *Identity Collage* be treated as *unconditional preternatural opportunity:* appreciated as beauty (art object) and entered as one would an ashram or cave for the sake of carrying forth pertinent work.

Incense is wafting; opera is playing, loud enough to shake the windows. I am planting red things on the brink. Is this a form of self-made storm?

Some of these works were created in the red light of what I call *My Cave* (a small workshop area in my basement). Some of them were created in the cubicle at my job when everyone else had long gone home. There are still glue marks on my desk, colors pressed into my fingerprints.

In a cave, it is dark. This darkness enables a he and a she to share a body in ways that are not at all at odds with one another. This is not necessarily a male he; this is not necessarily a female she. Are these lovers? Are they two of many aspects of a singular, the myriad in singularity?

Touch and union predate distinction. Instead of being a historicized weapon, in a cave a pronoun can be a validating *reflection*, the experience of reverberation, a place in which staring can occur. When an umbilical state *is* our sense of place (as with a cave), is the zone by which we mature a visual version of tone?

Within the cave they abound. They are dangling from walls and ceiling, from the cells of inhabitants: handmade collages made out of found images and paint. In some cases, these pieces were made by shadow-box method which involved wood and nails and pins. The only unflinching standard I want extant in these works is an undeniable *mystical lucidness.*

It is my intention that lucidity be capable of swallowing up and enabling any-one who enters—much like a trance would enable.

Glands and organs are being offered opportunities toward rites of passage. The folds are being ghosted. Round rooms are recognized as additive-wombs: new sights by which to birth unforeseen animals, myriad maximums, sonorous smears.

A hand-made cave in which *Identity Collage* thrives is flamboyant, is the flab-lab. In the flab-lab there is material hope for a new kind of merge. Merge is a radical activism that radiates us.

While working with caves I always try to practice a form of circular breathing. Penetrate the cup of milk. Suck and blow at the same time as a way of holding the subliminal and the physical. The limbic system of sloughed light is contacted herein. Bells are ringing in an abounding psychic density.

Images are instruments in the making; images are never ultimatums. I cast enabling spells on so many implications. I weave and weave until something viscerally whole emerges from parts.

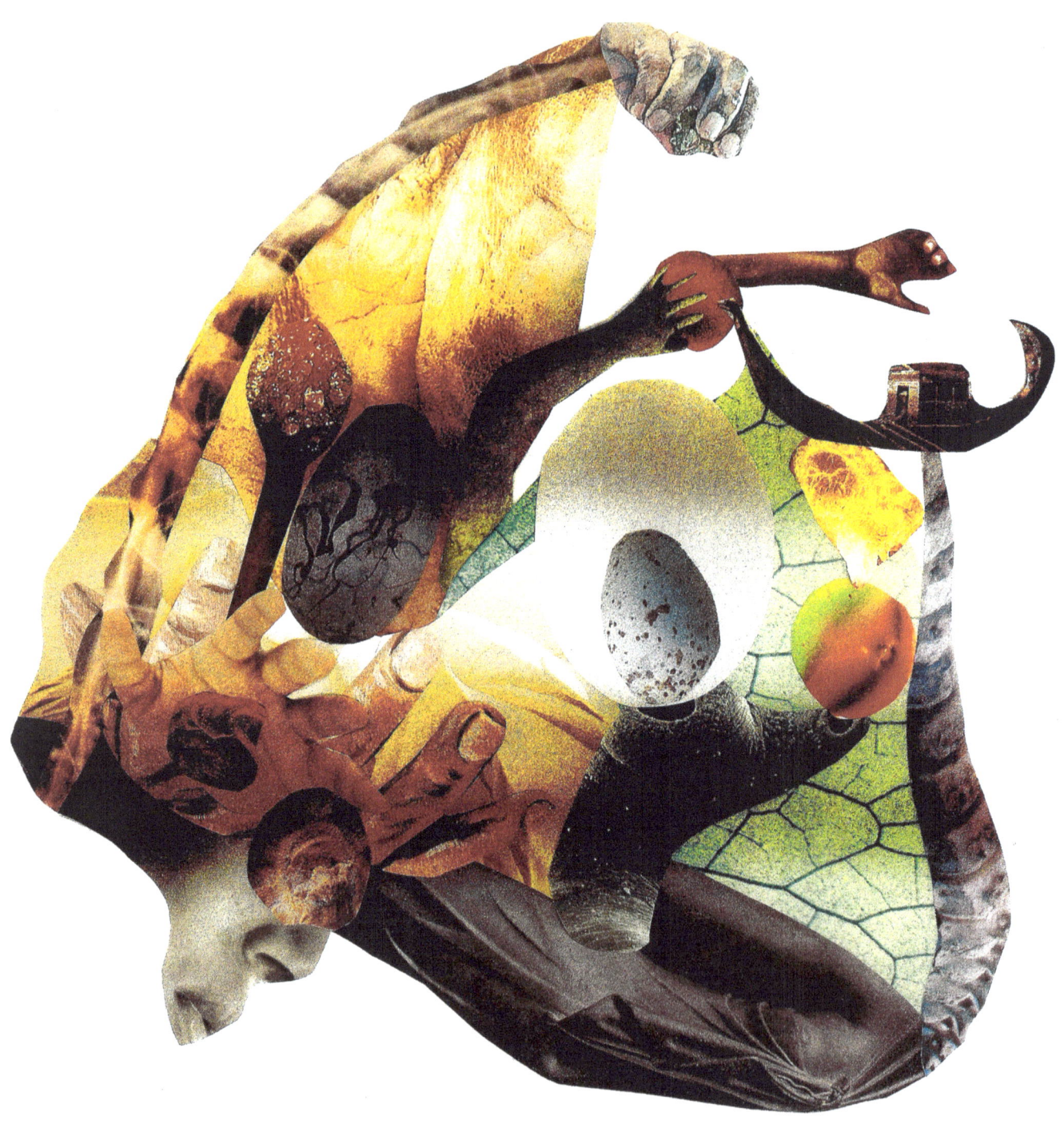

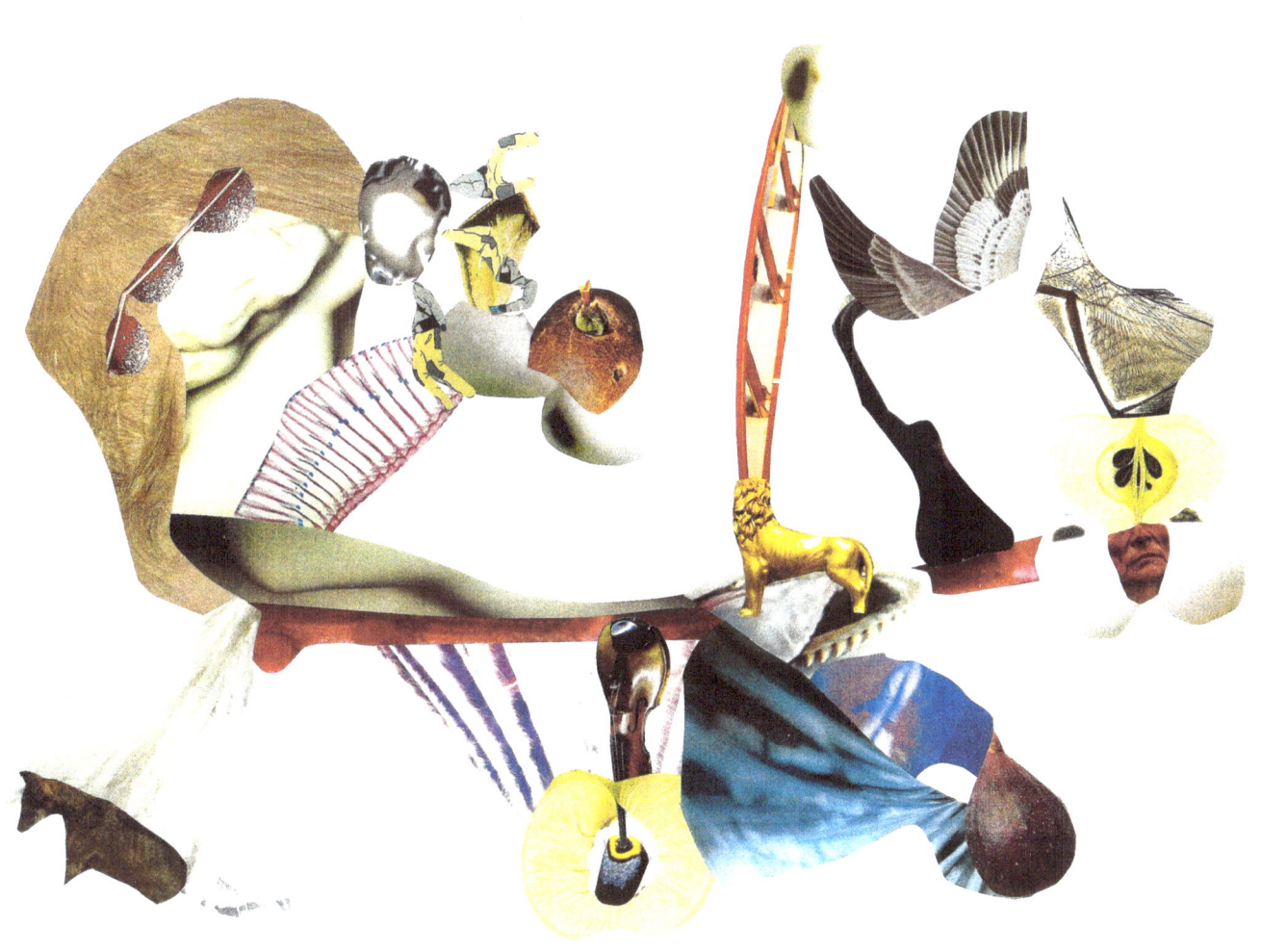

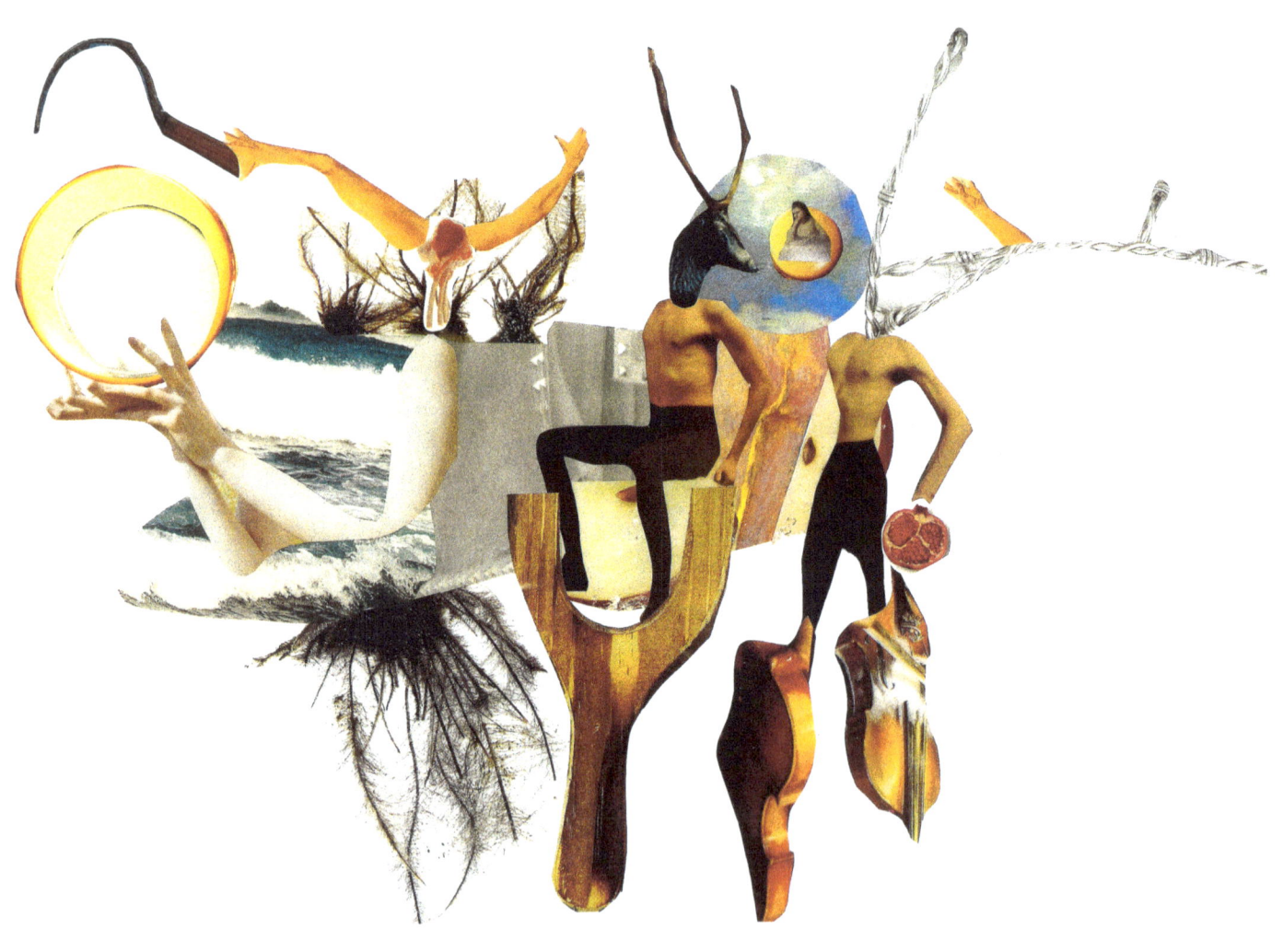

Swains

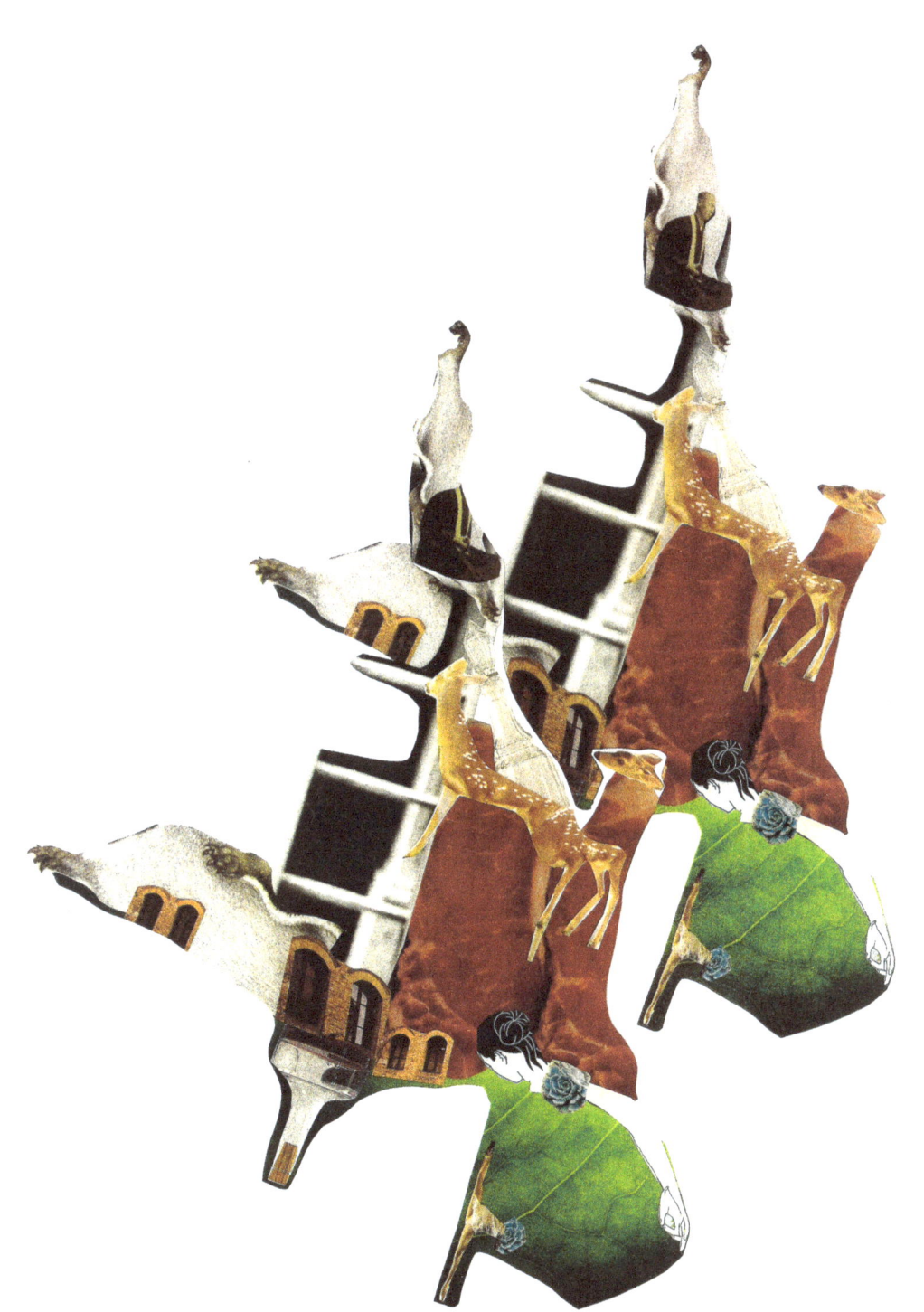

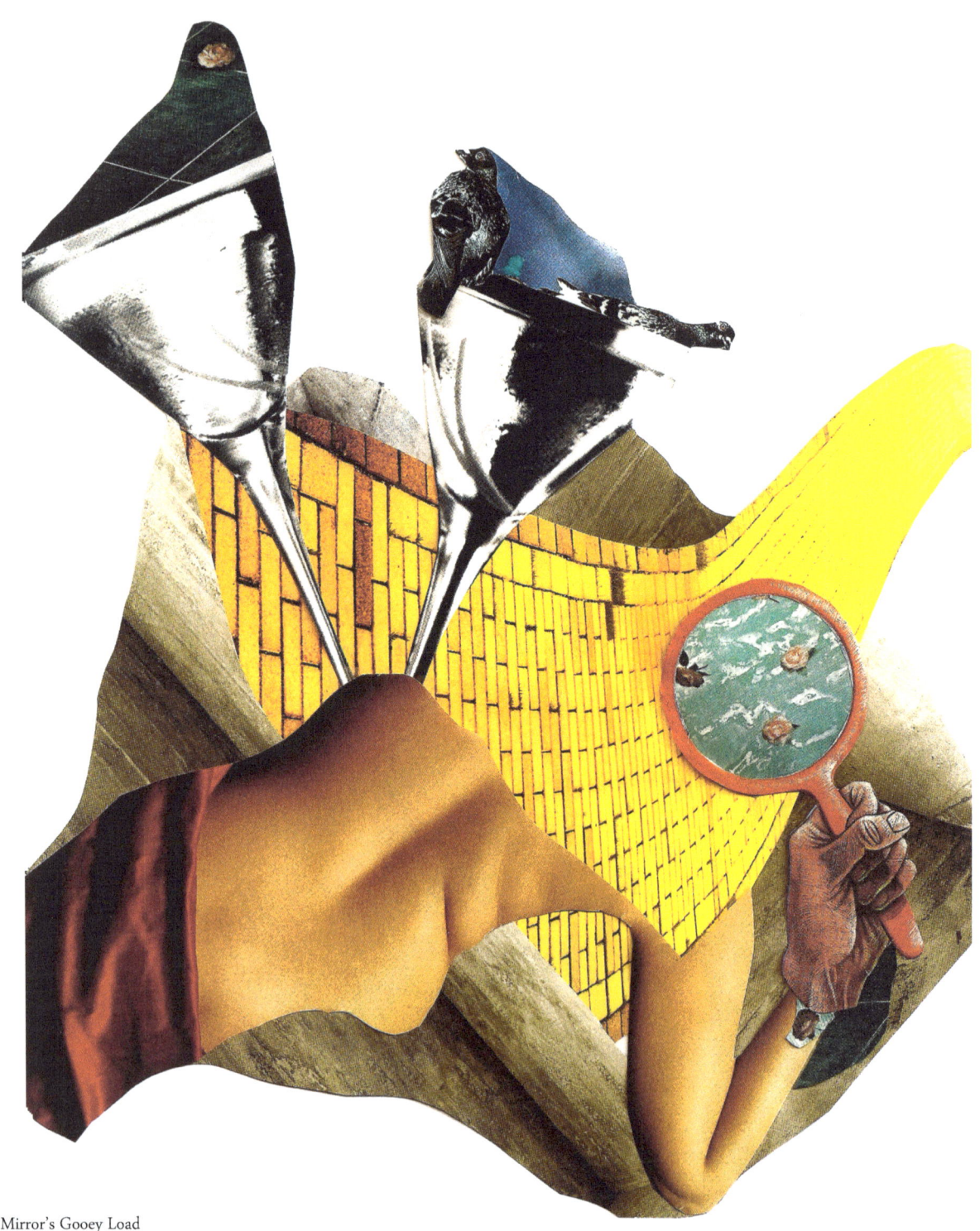

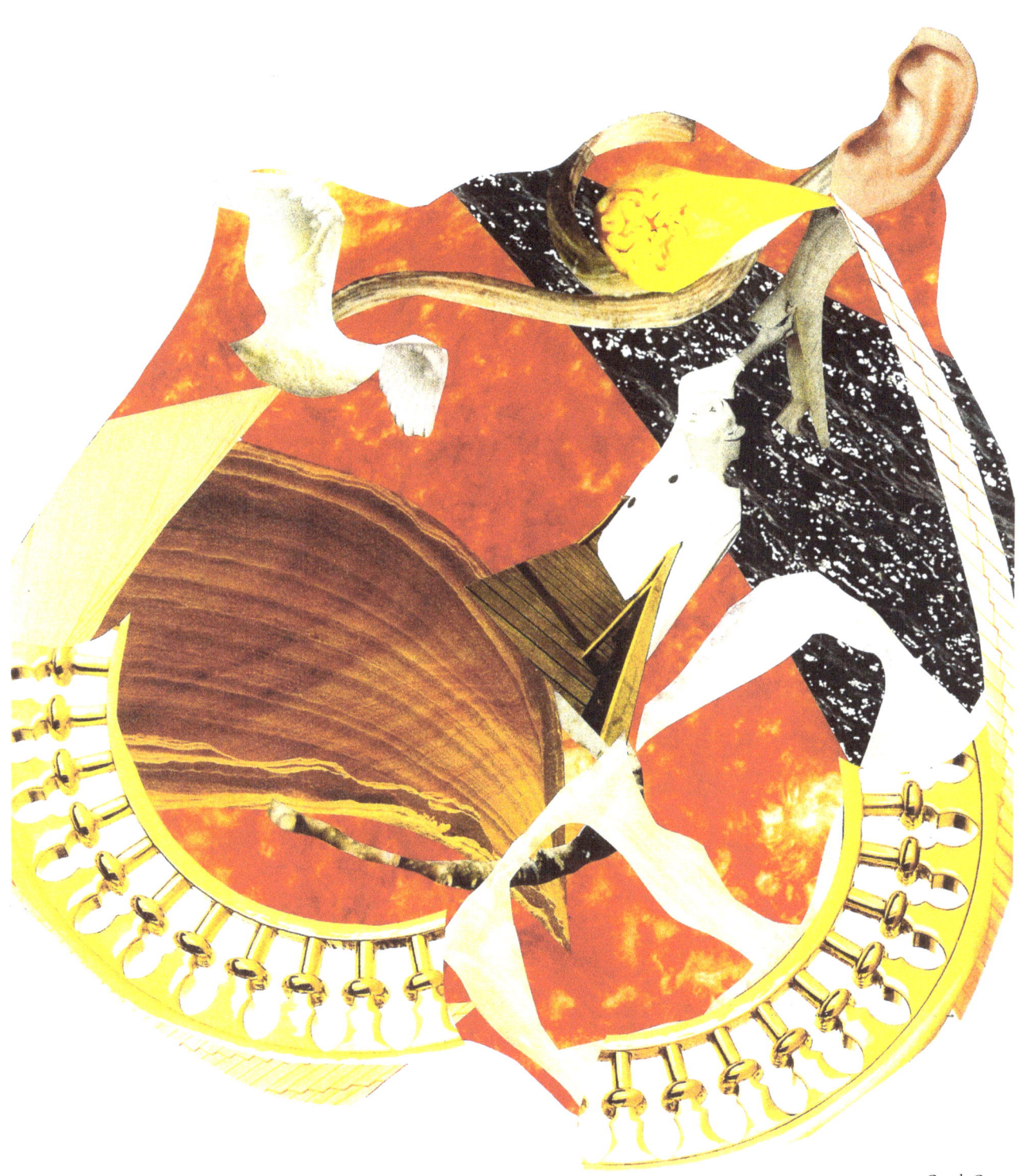

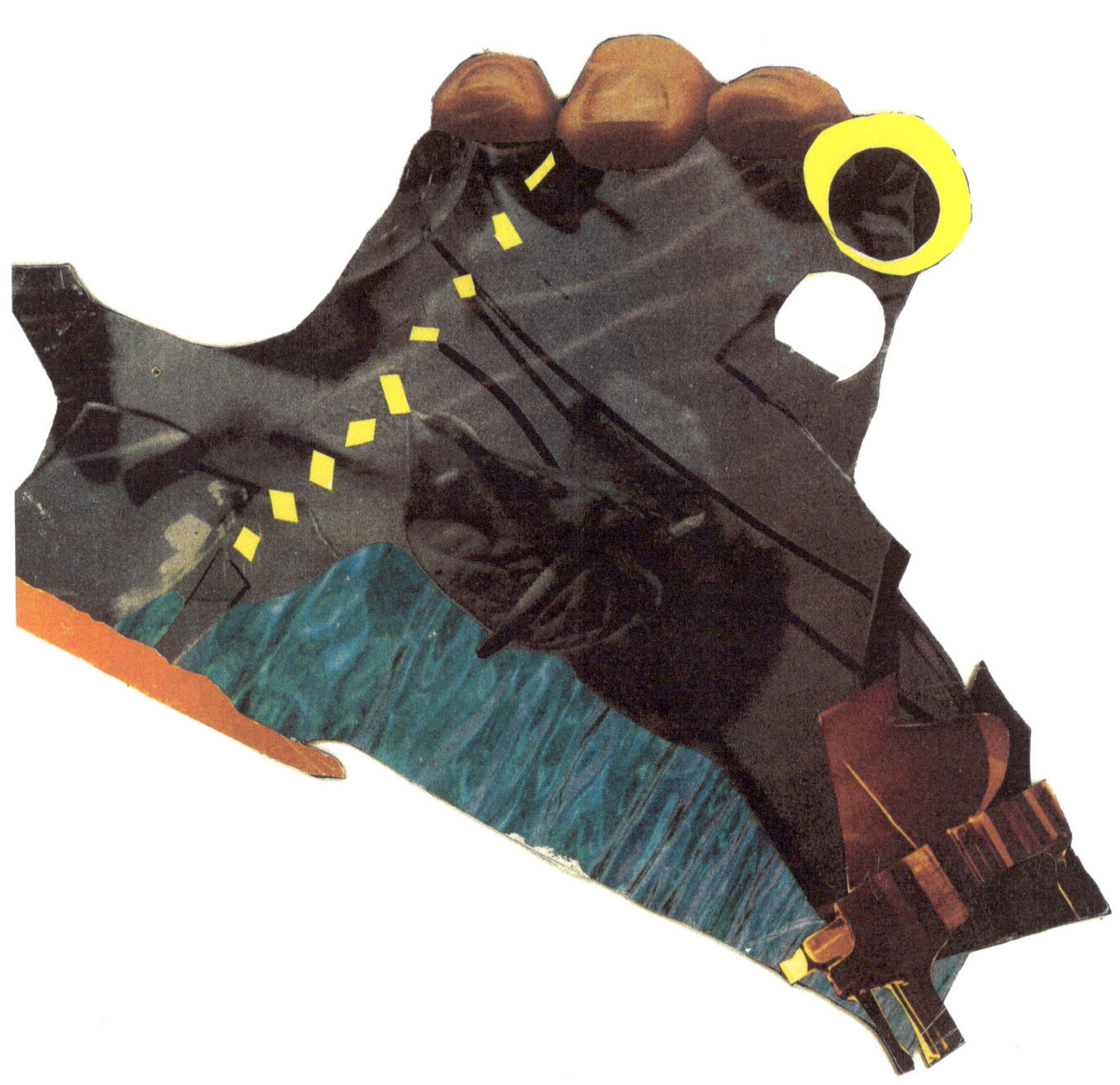

Hands As The First Voice

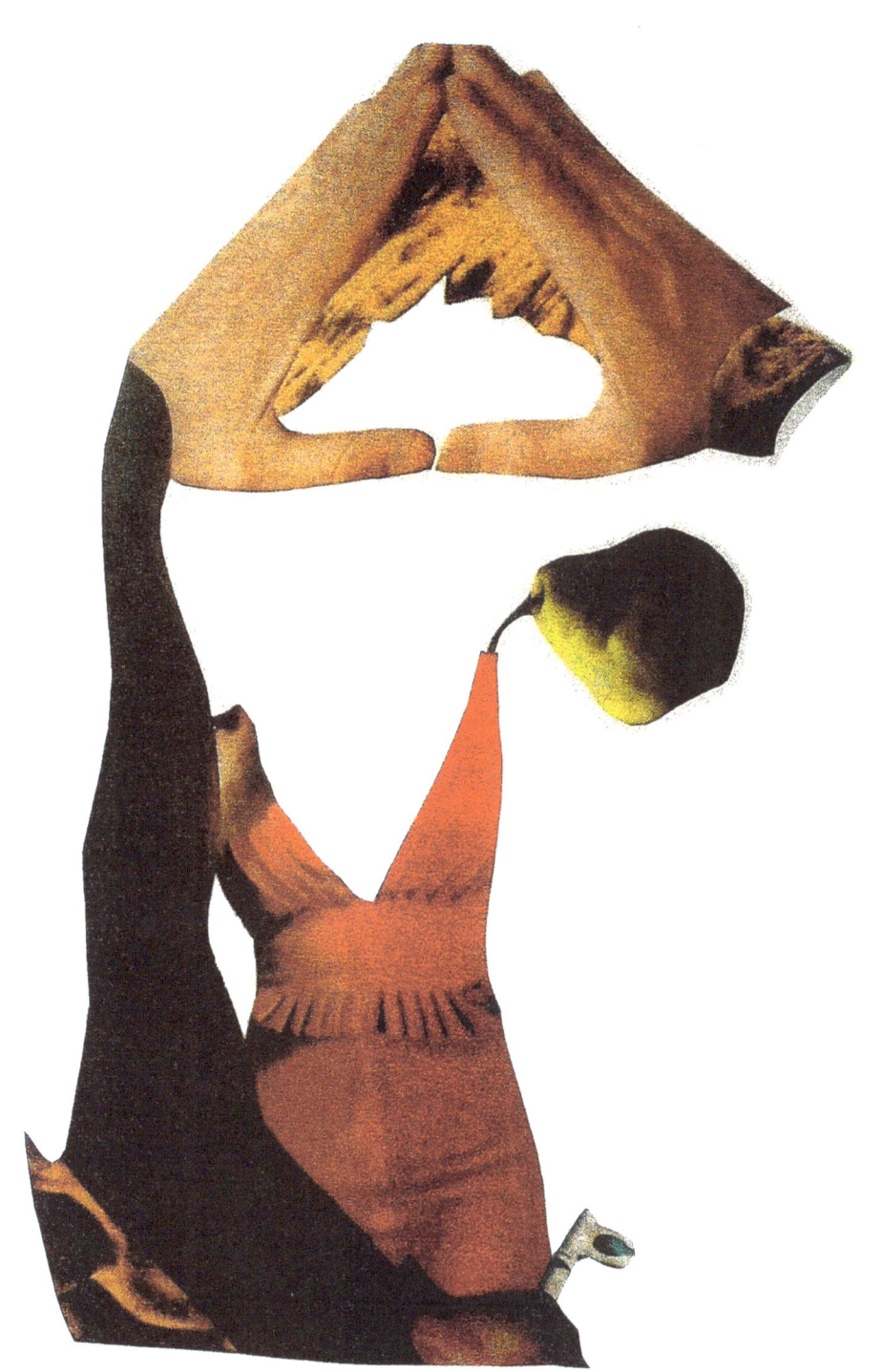

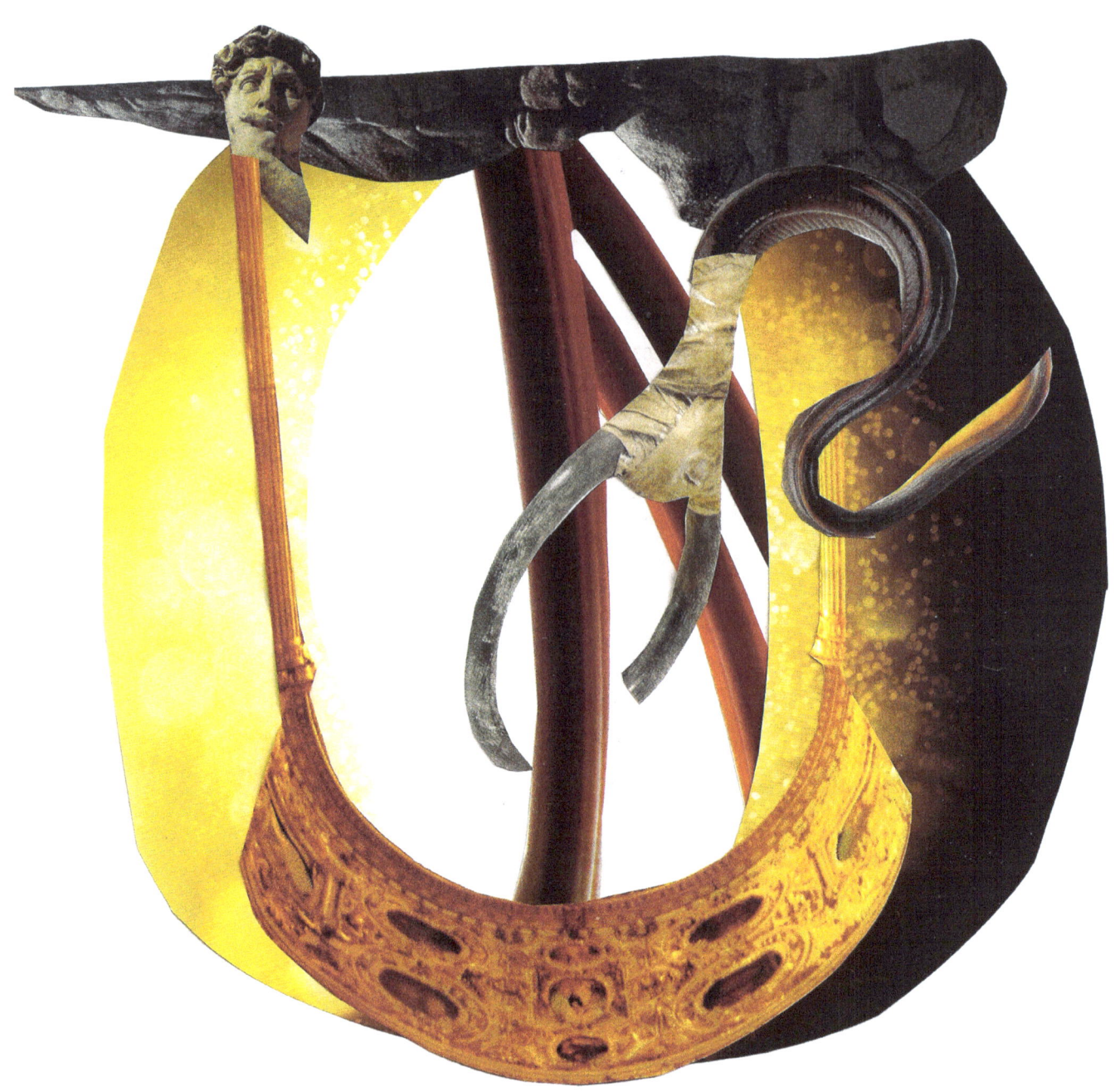

Curved Cleanse

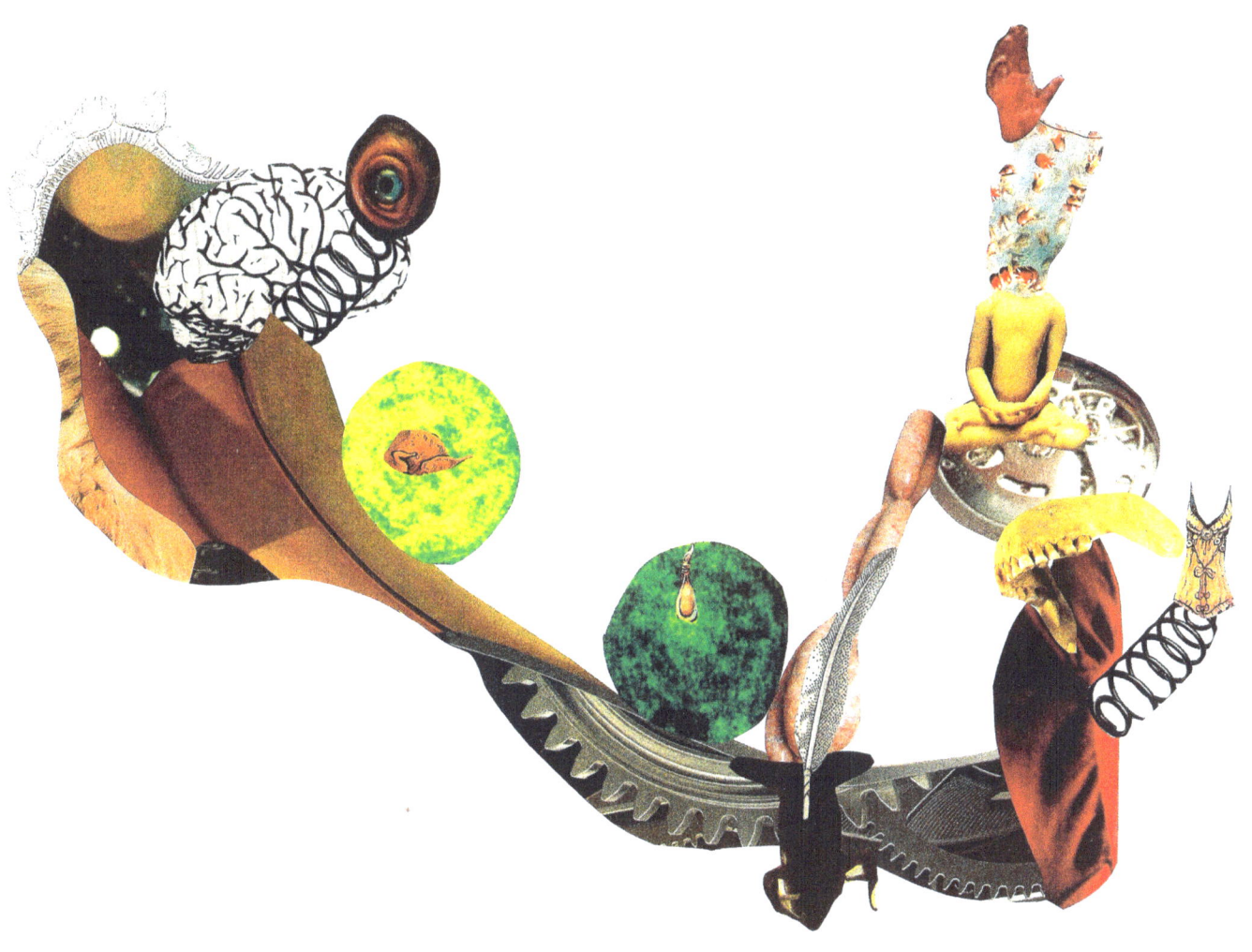

Frogs Changing Sexes   13

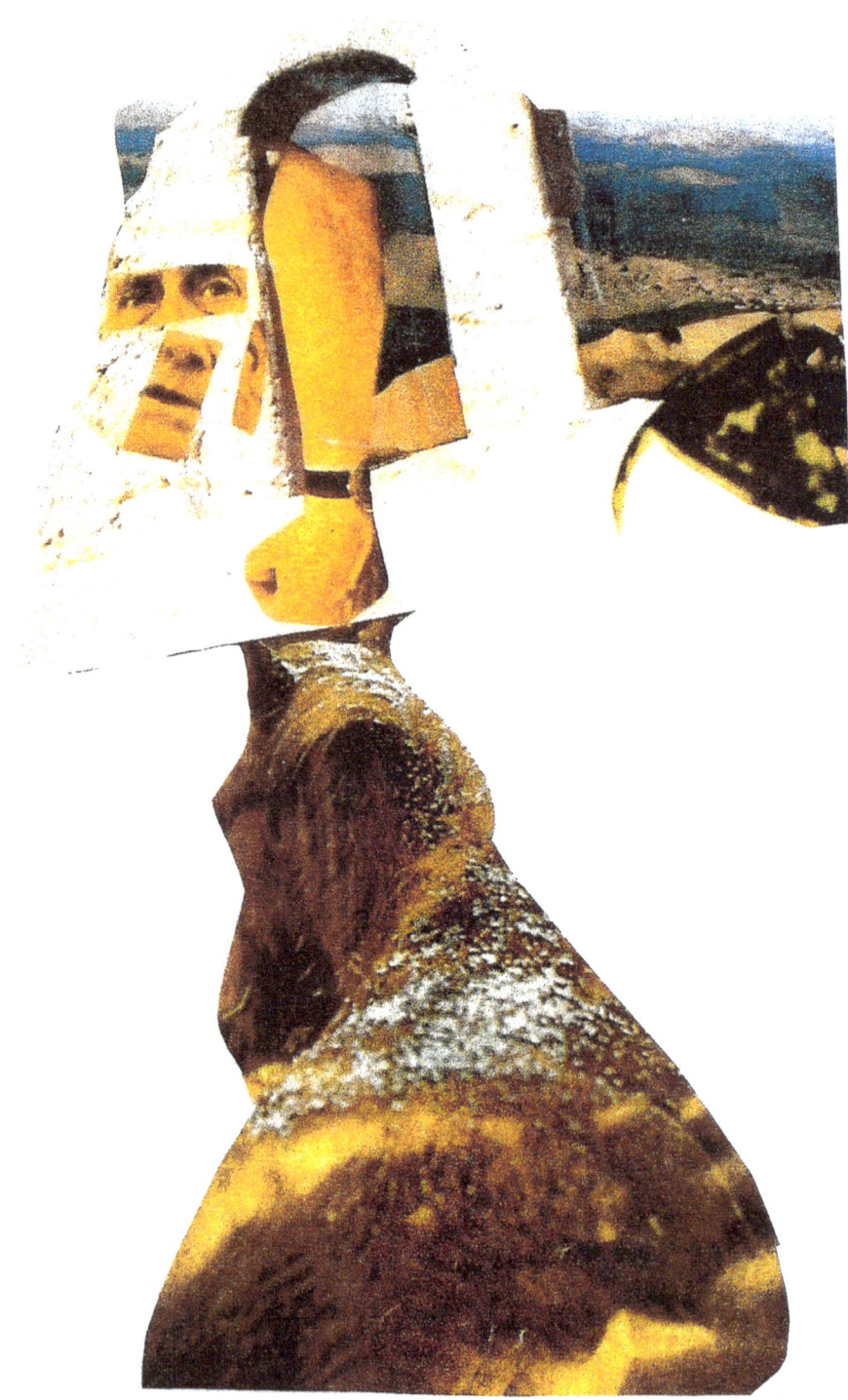

Butches Called Themselves Stallions/Grandpa's Hands

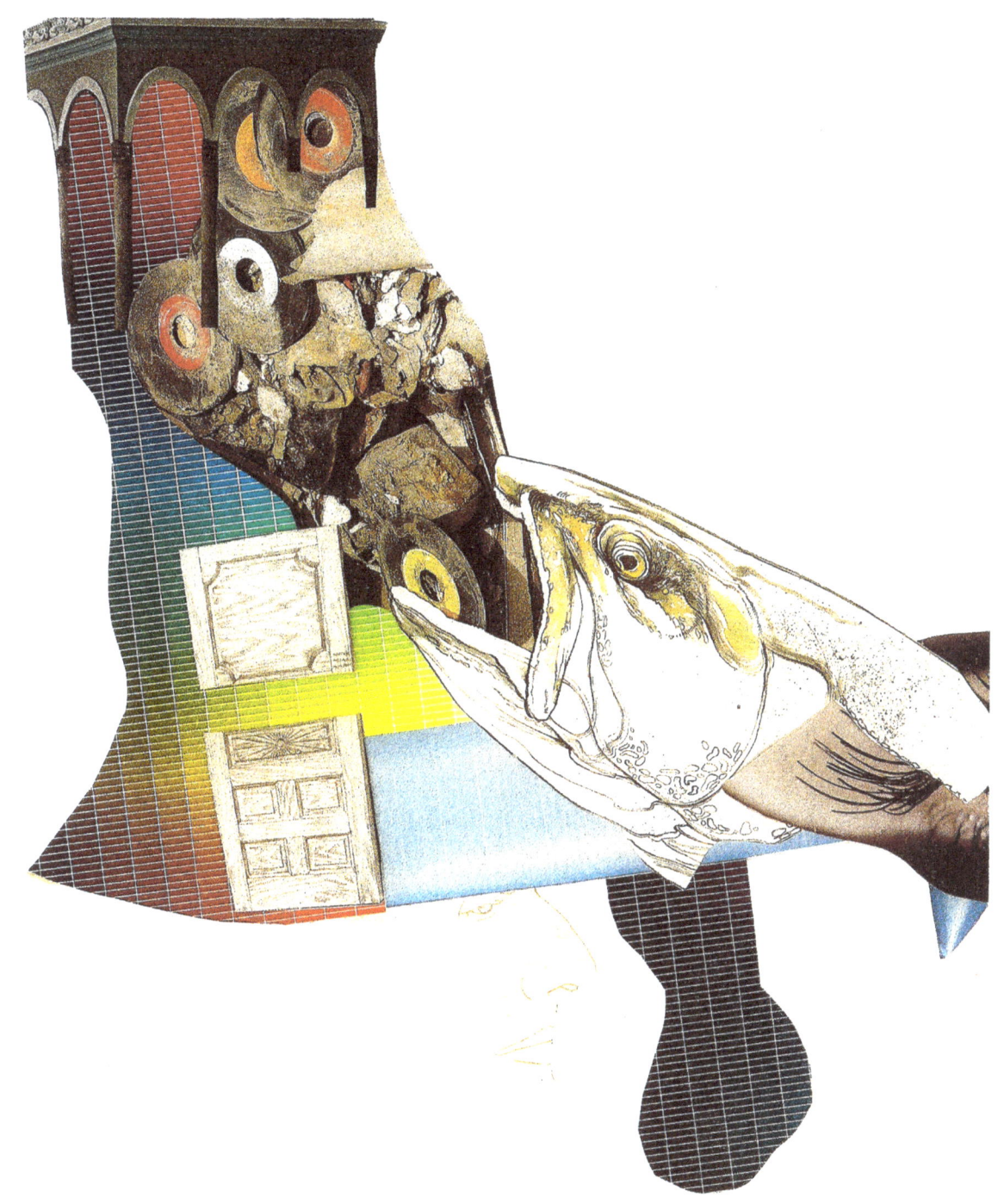

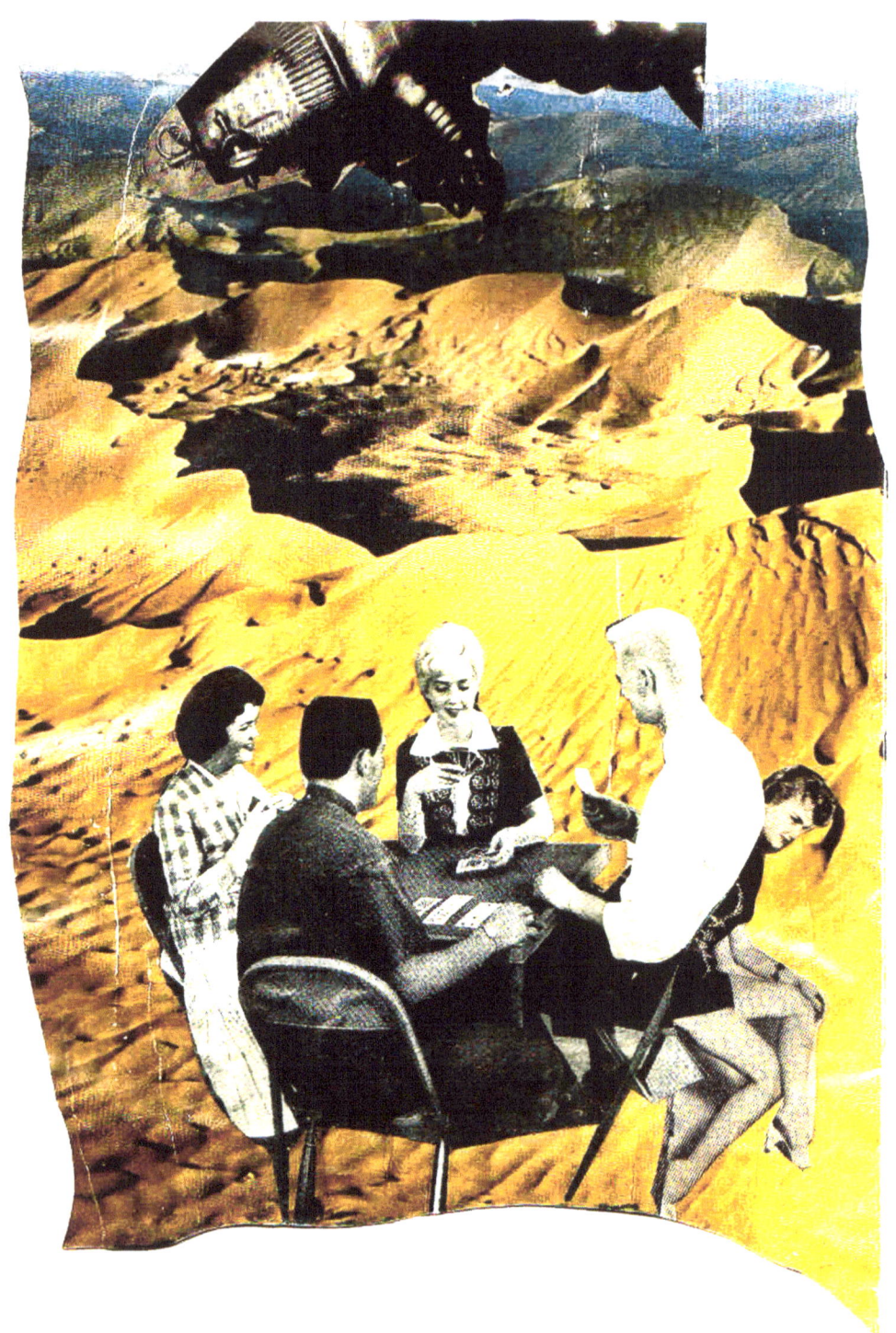

She Sits Beneath Him

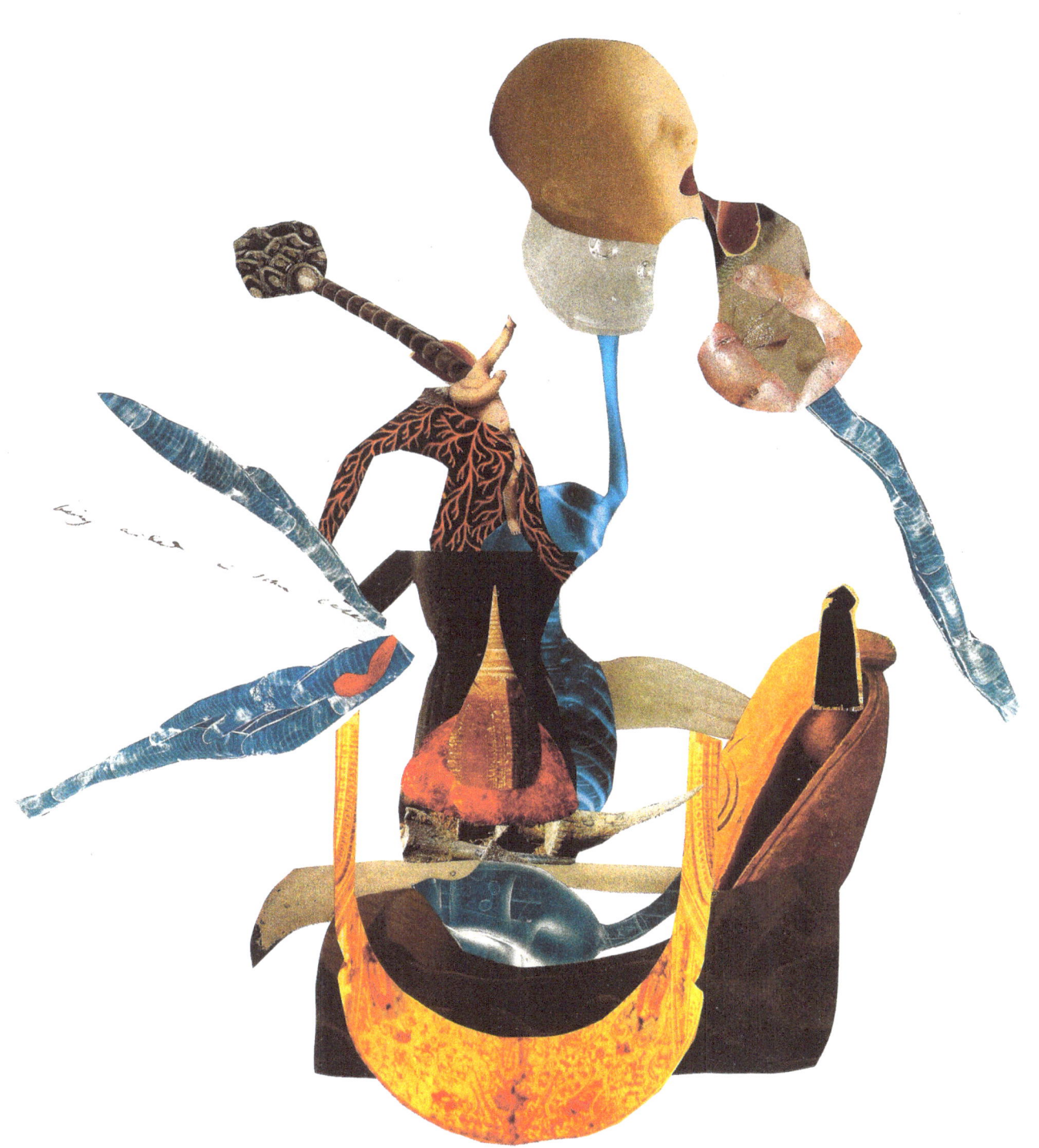

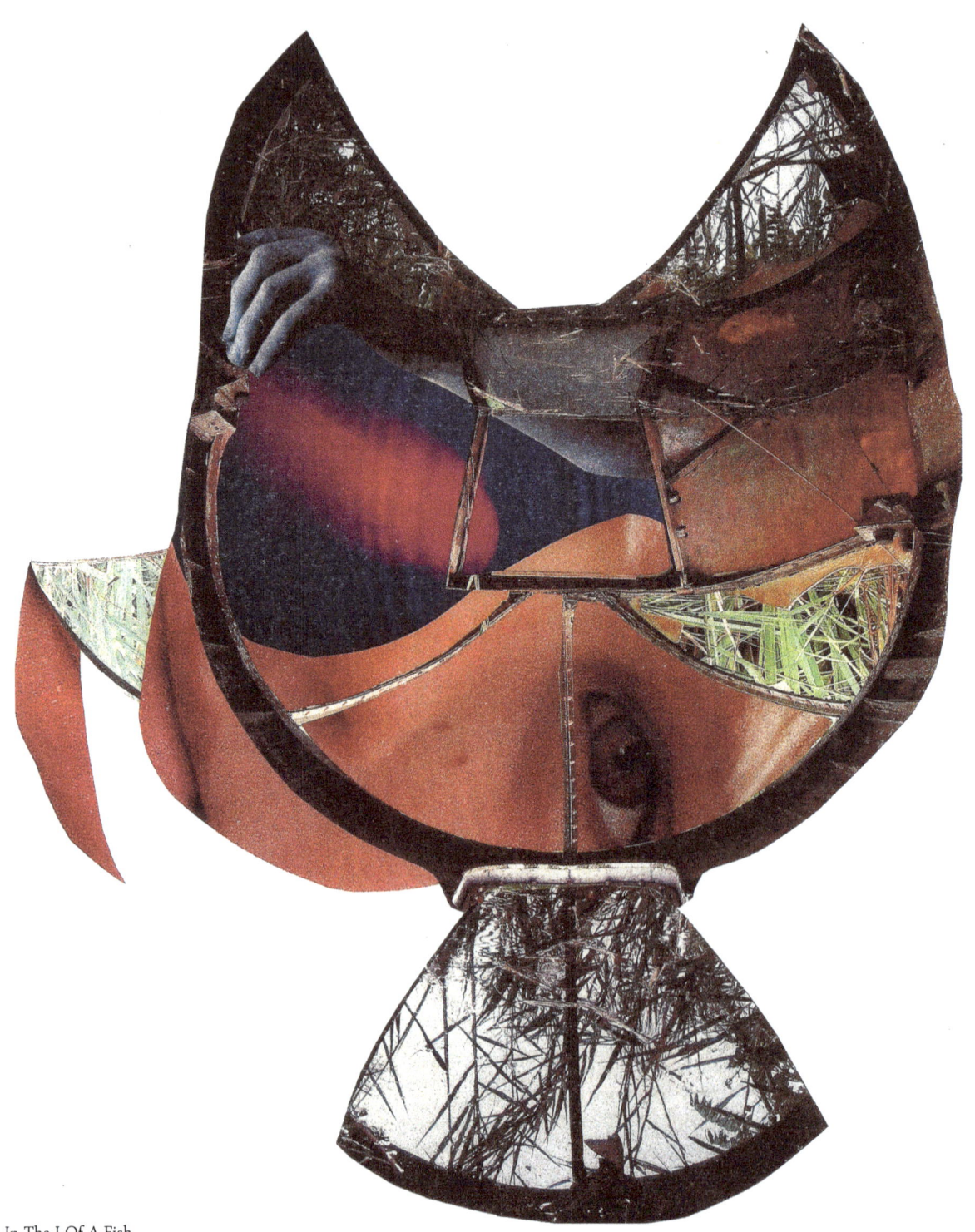

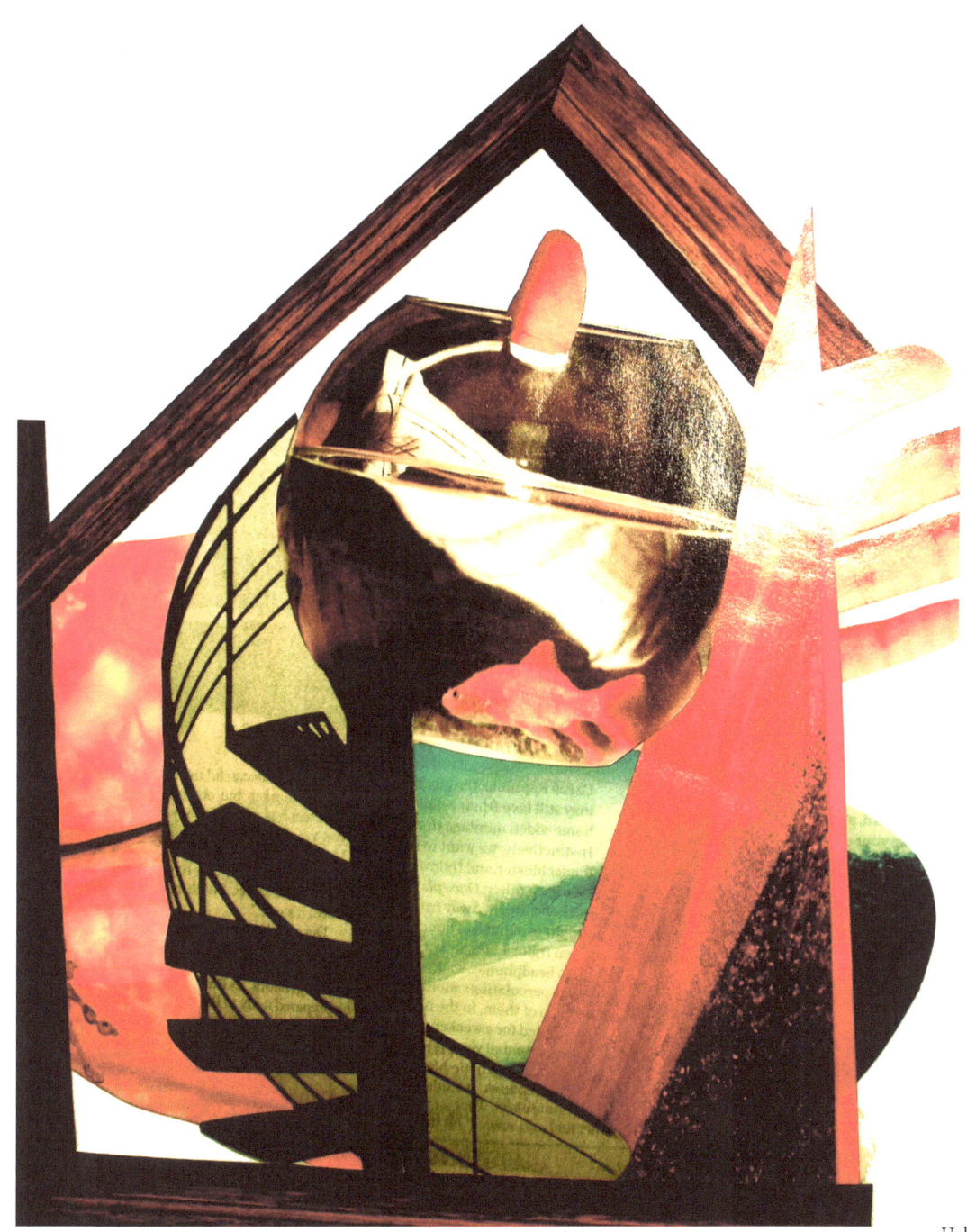

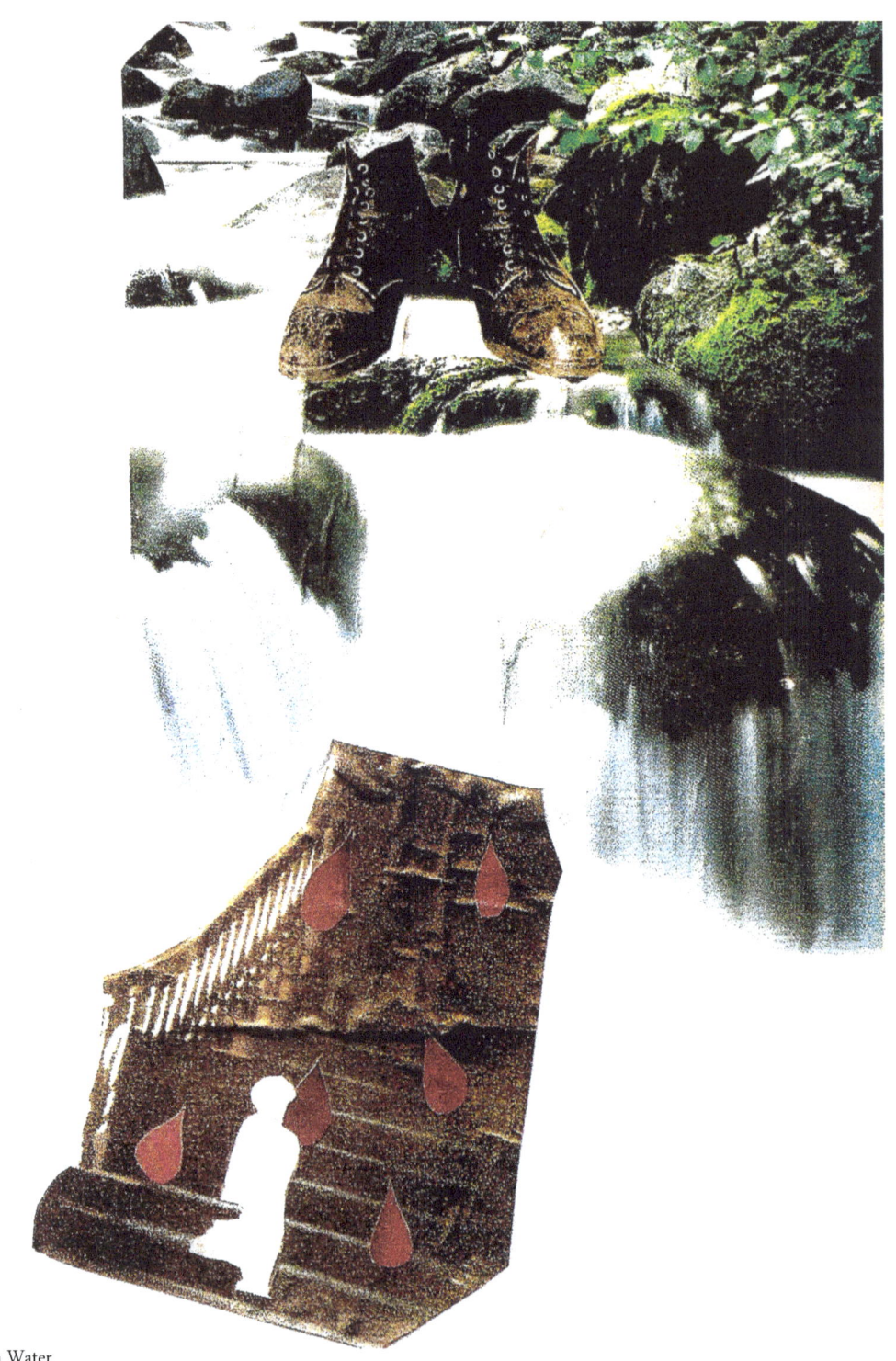

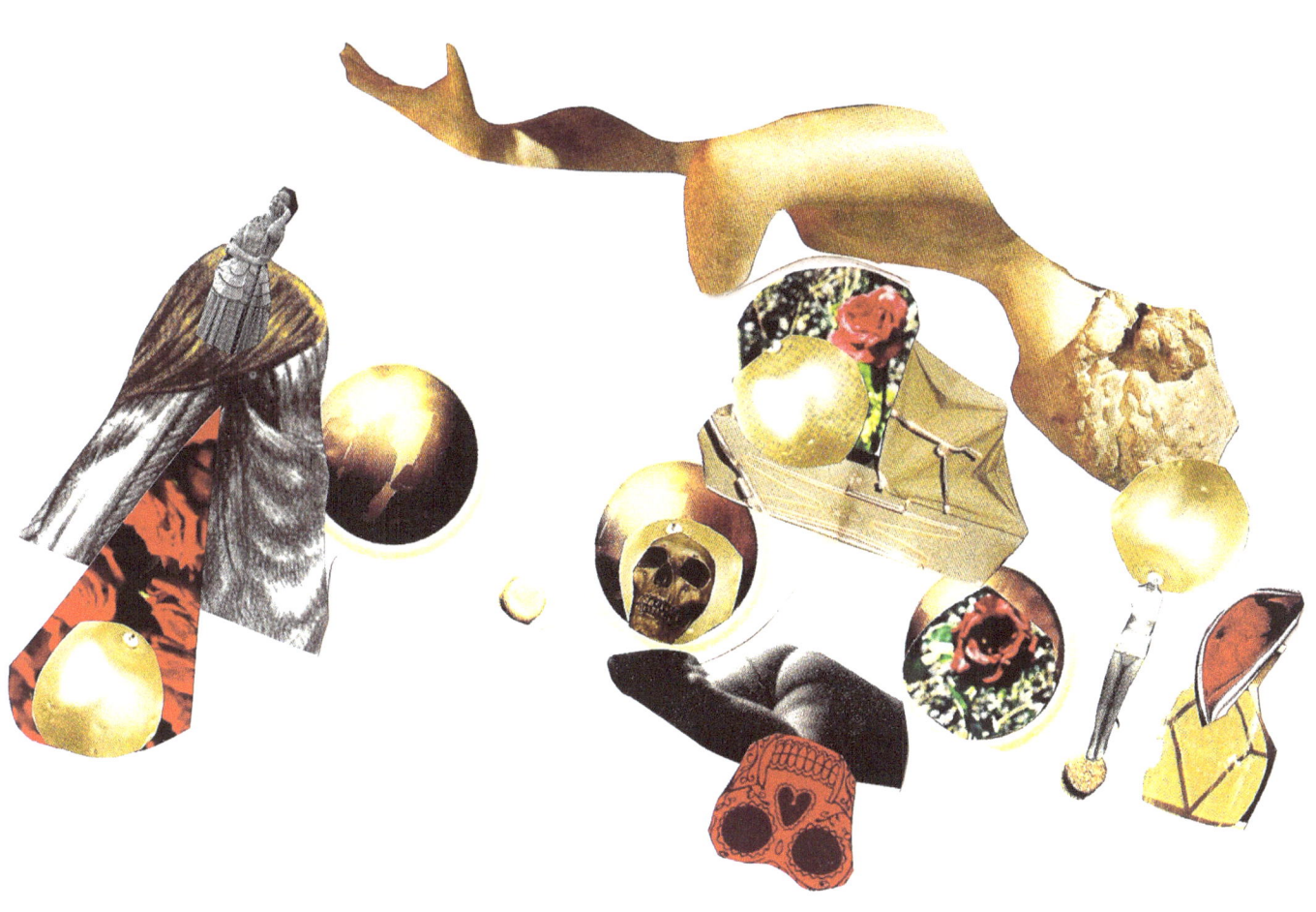

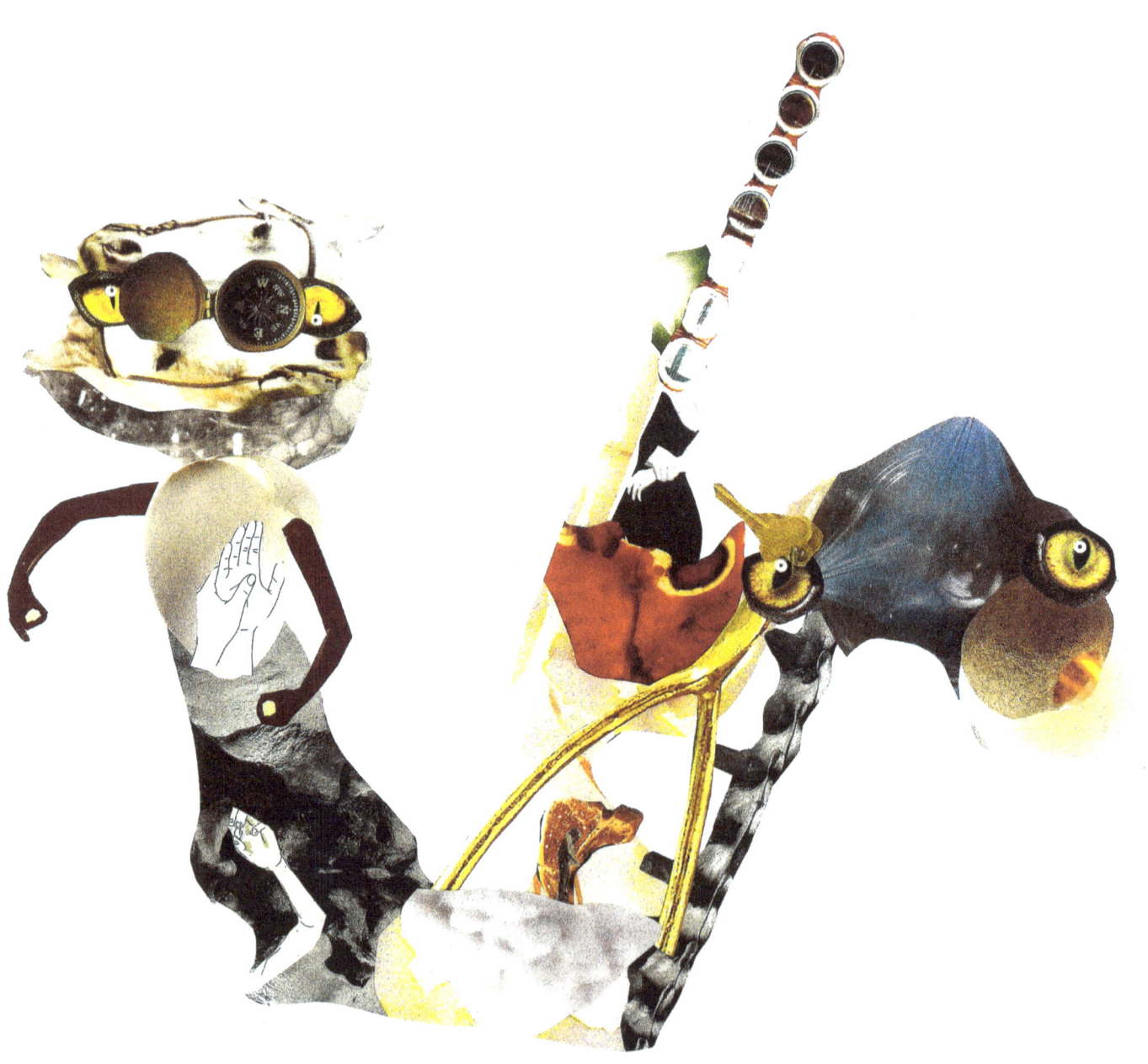

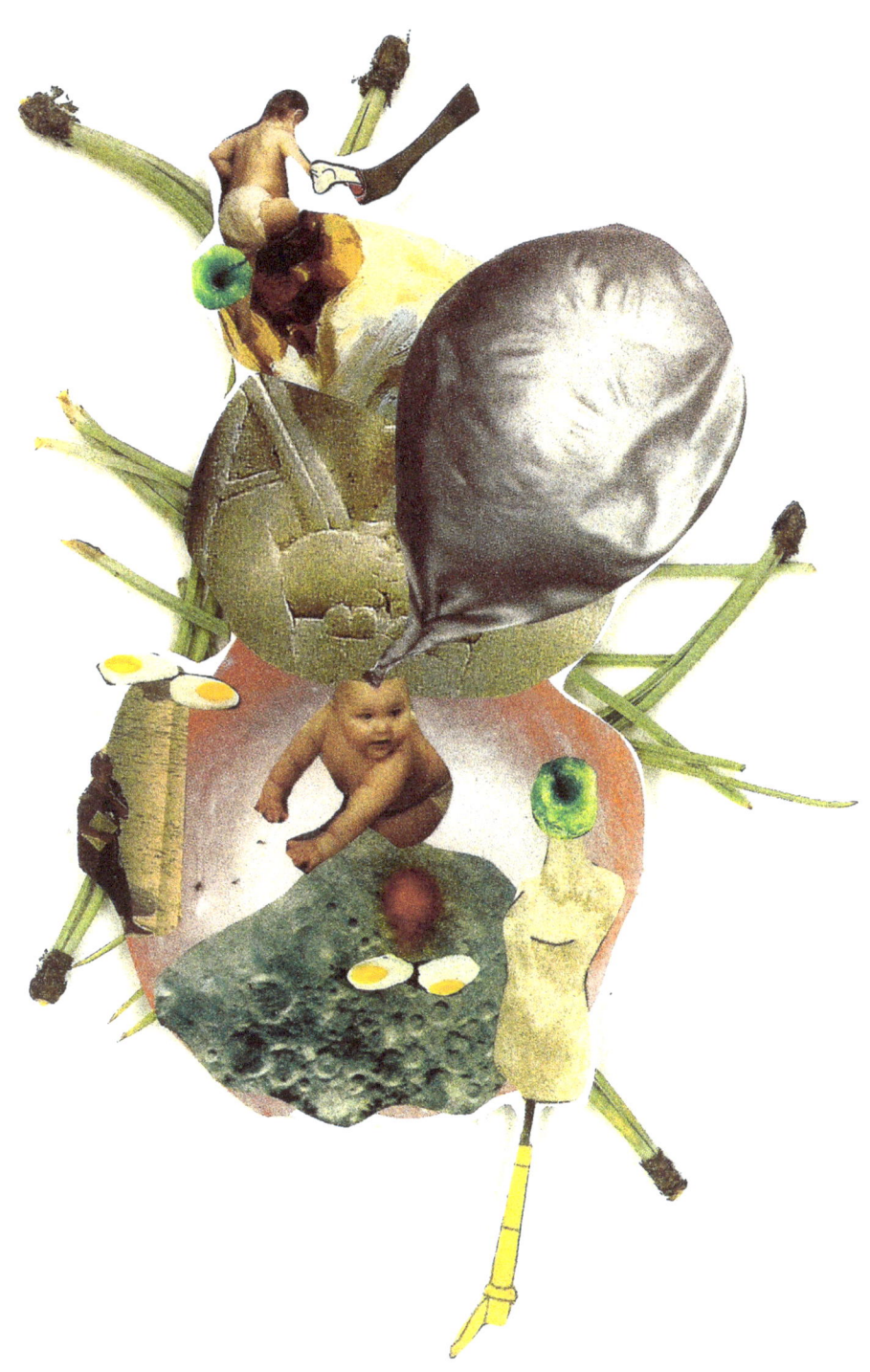

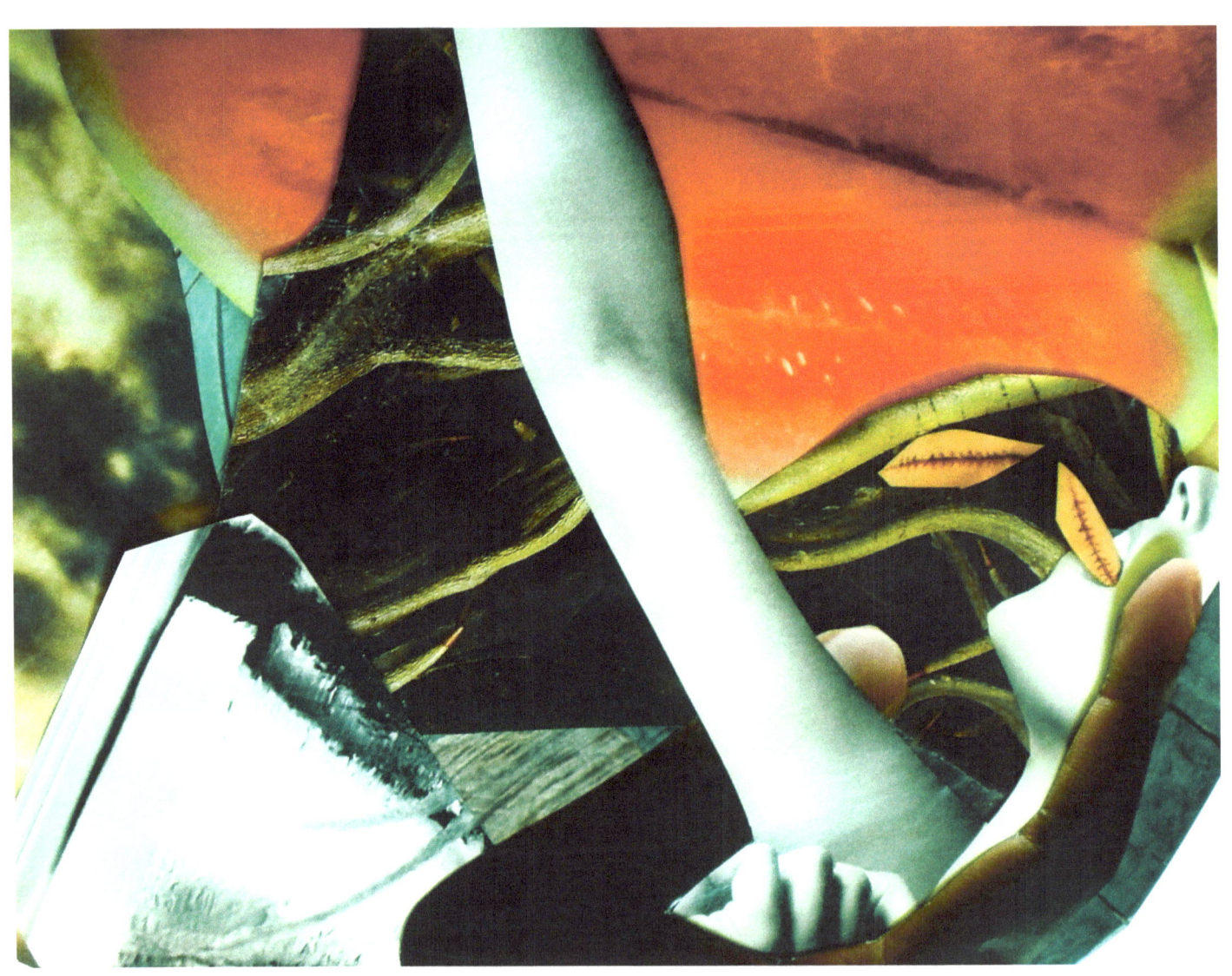

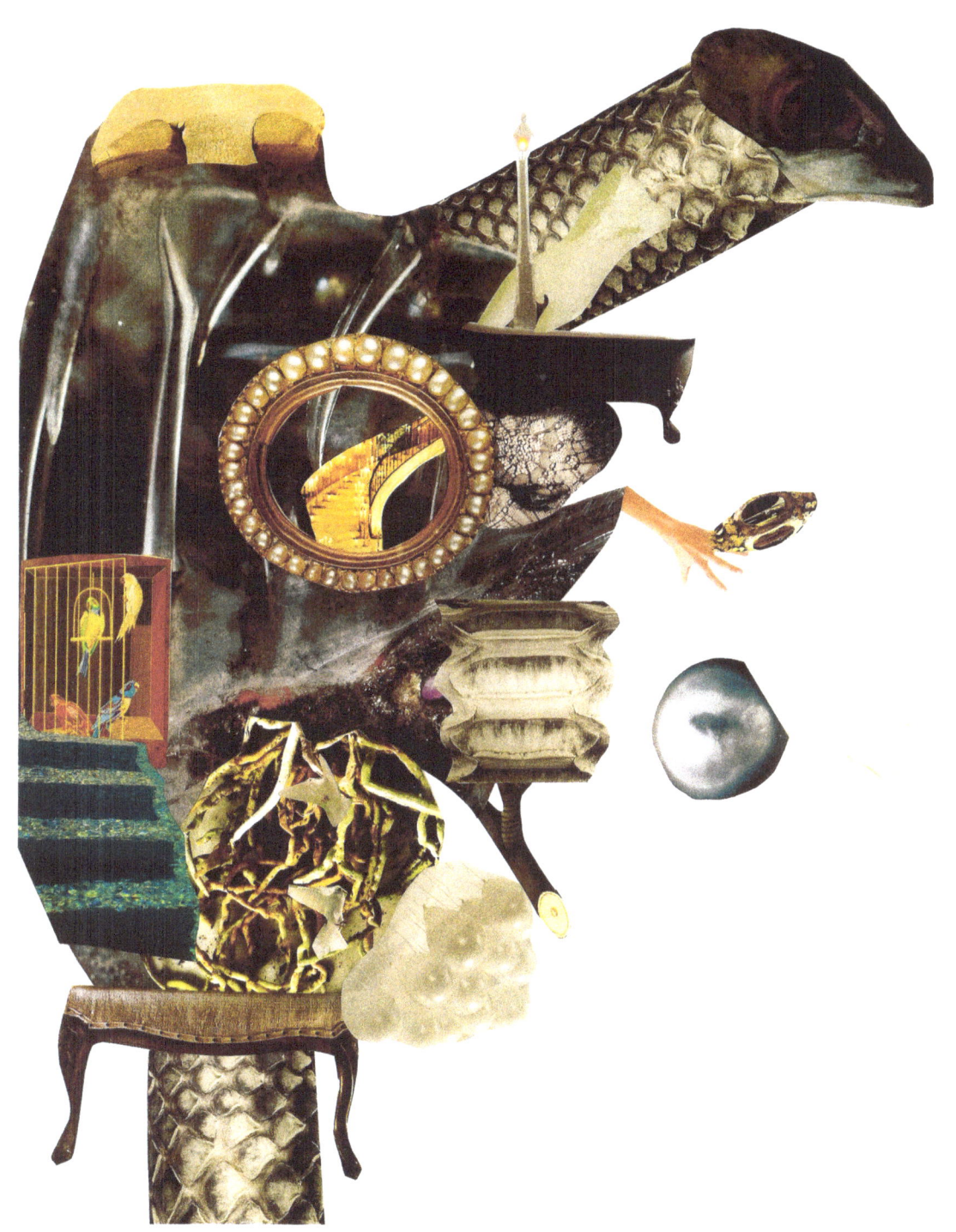

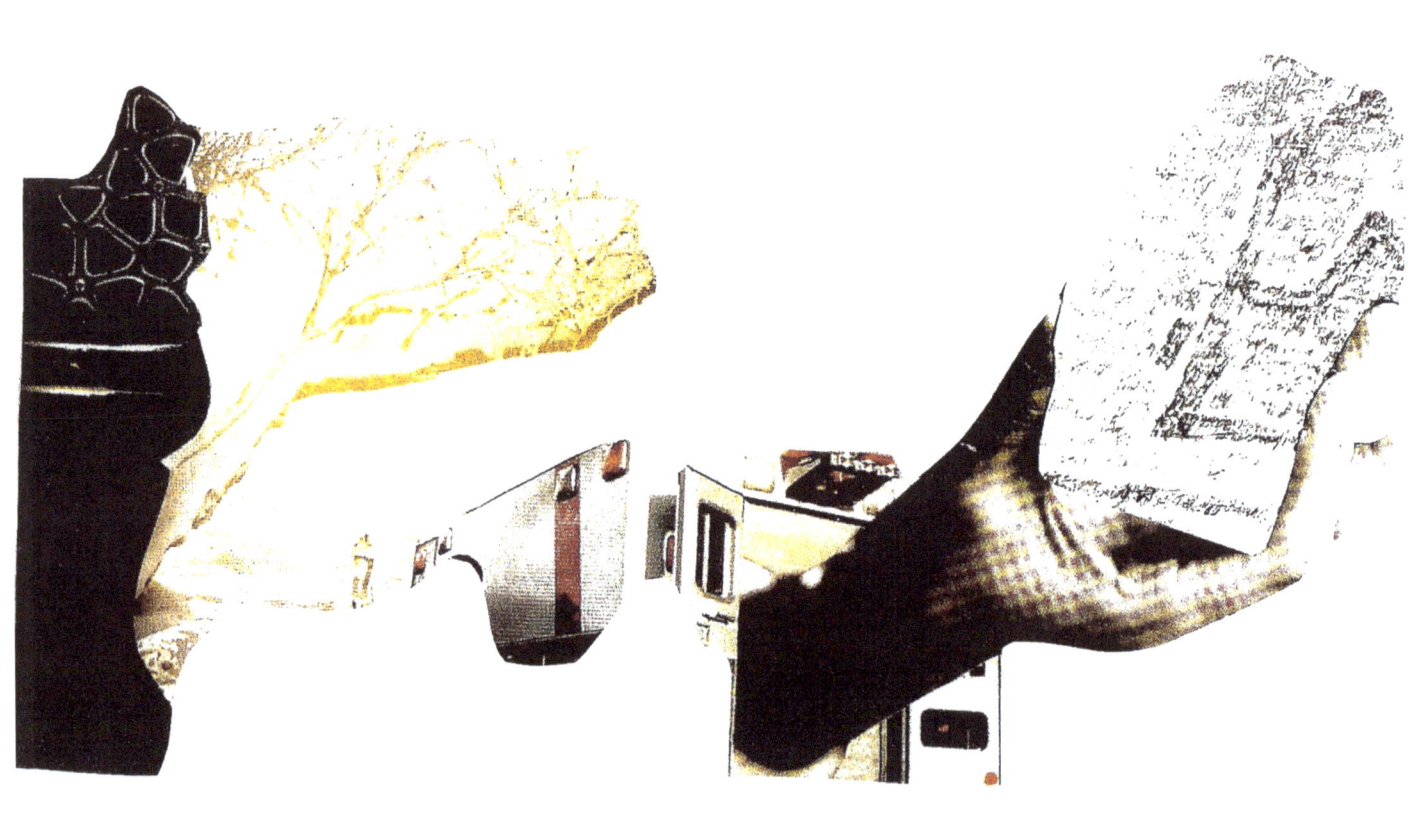

E

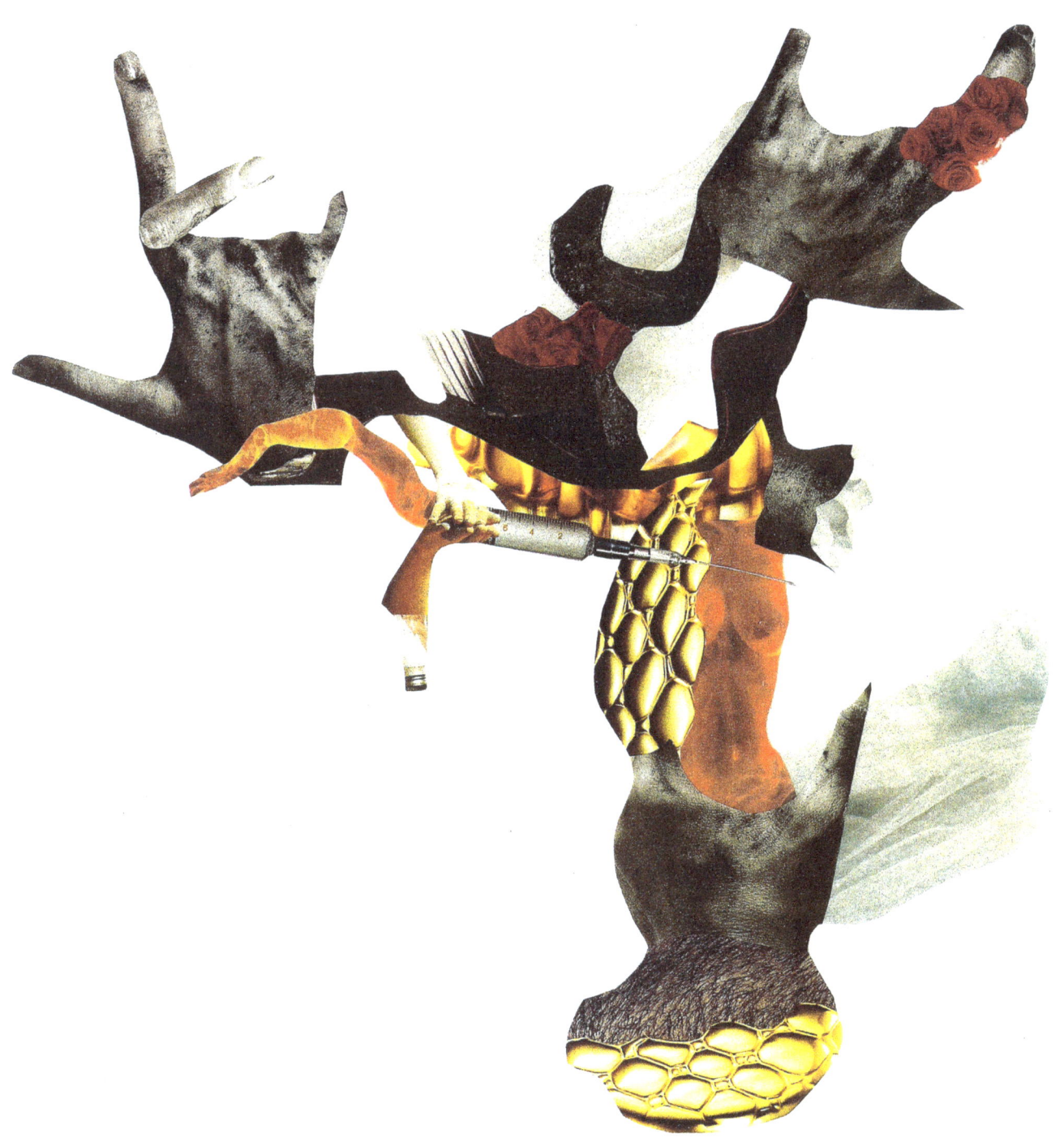

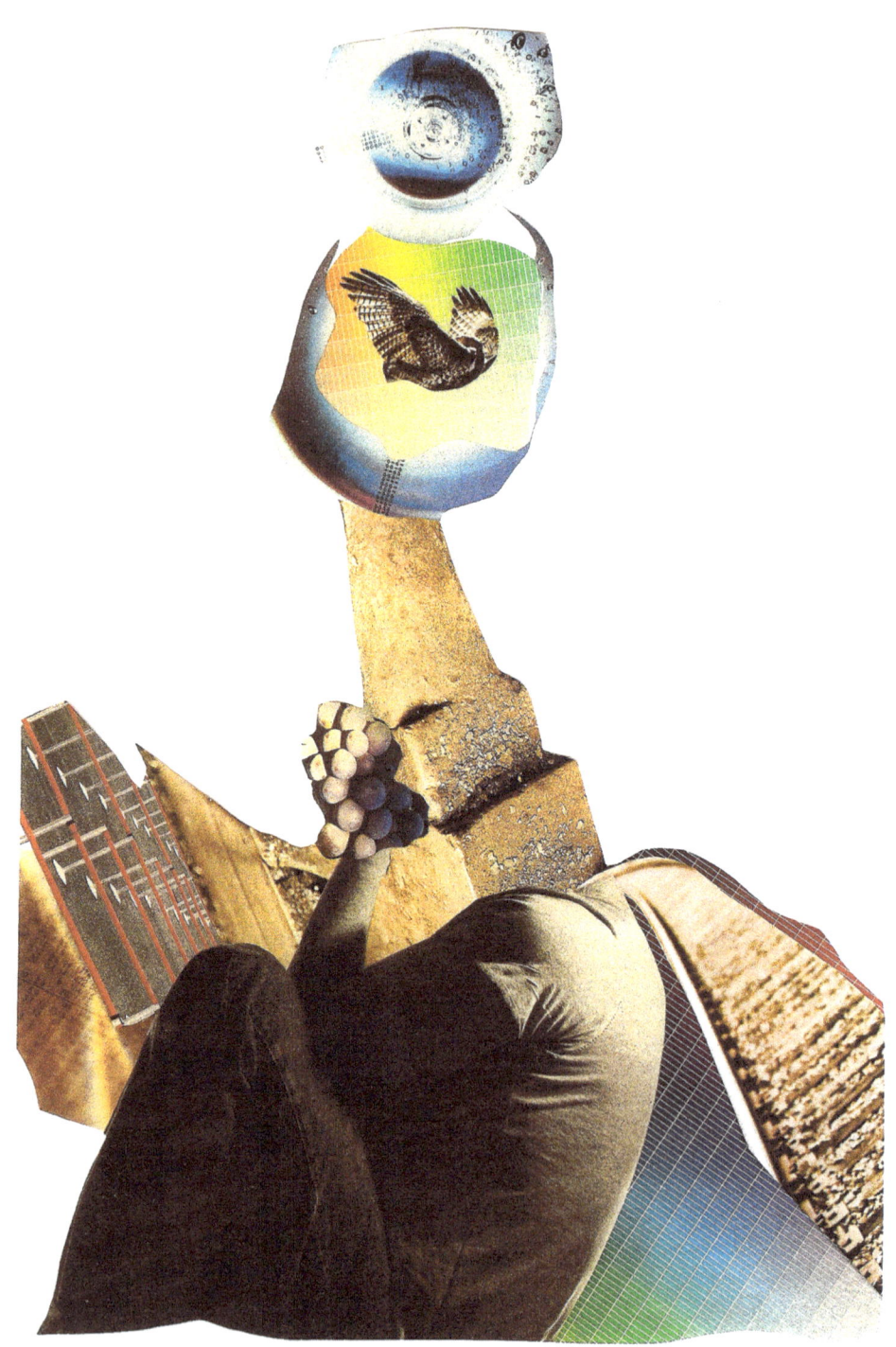

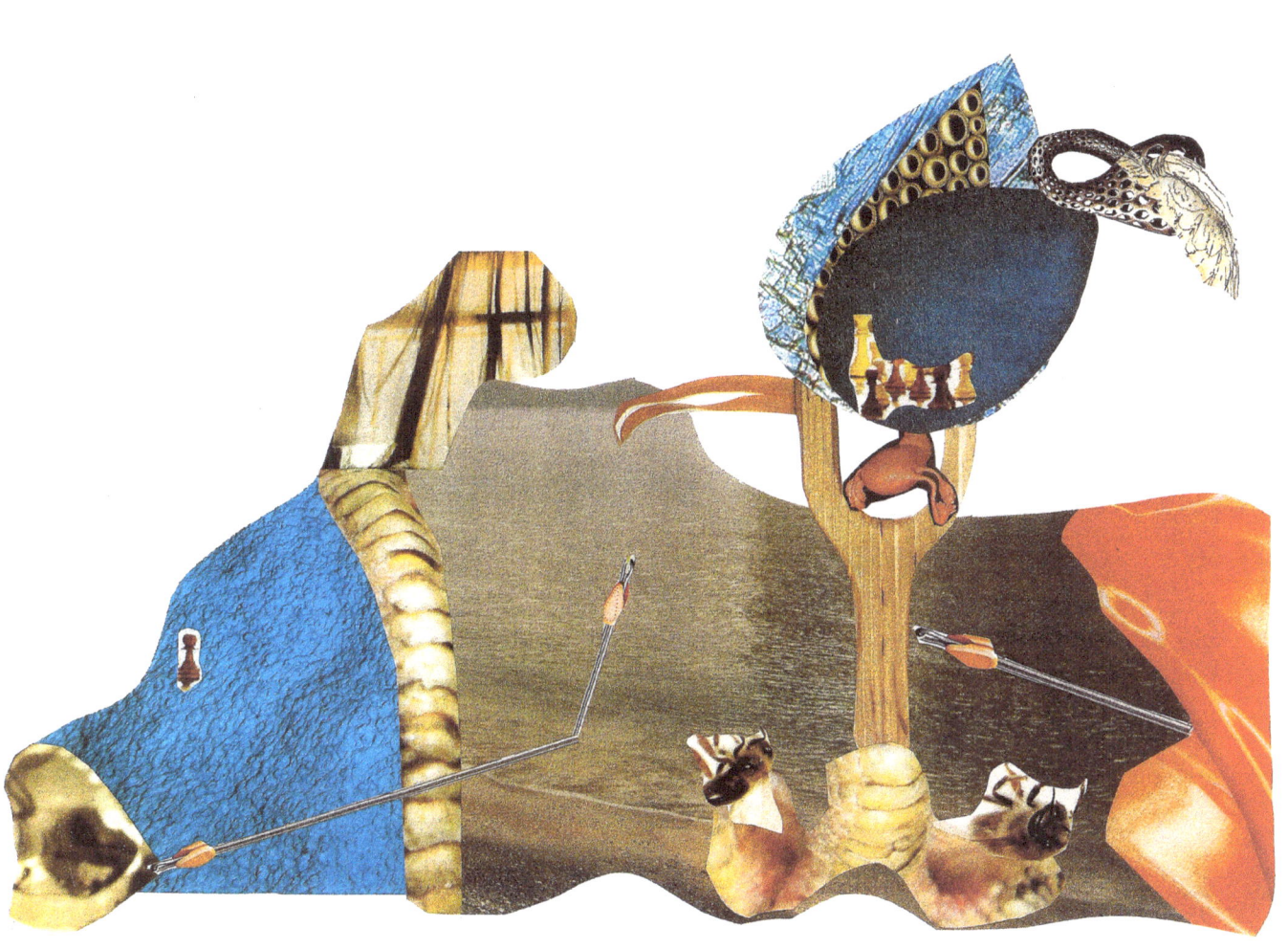

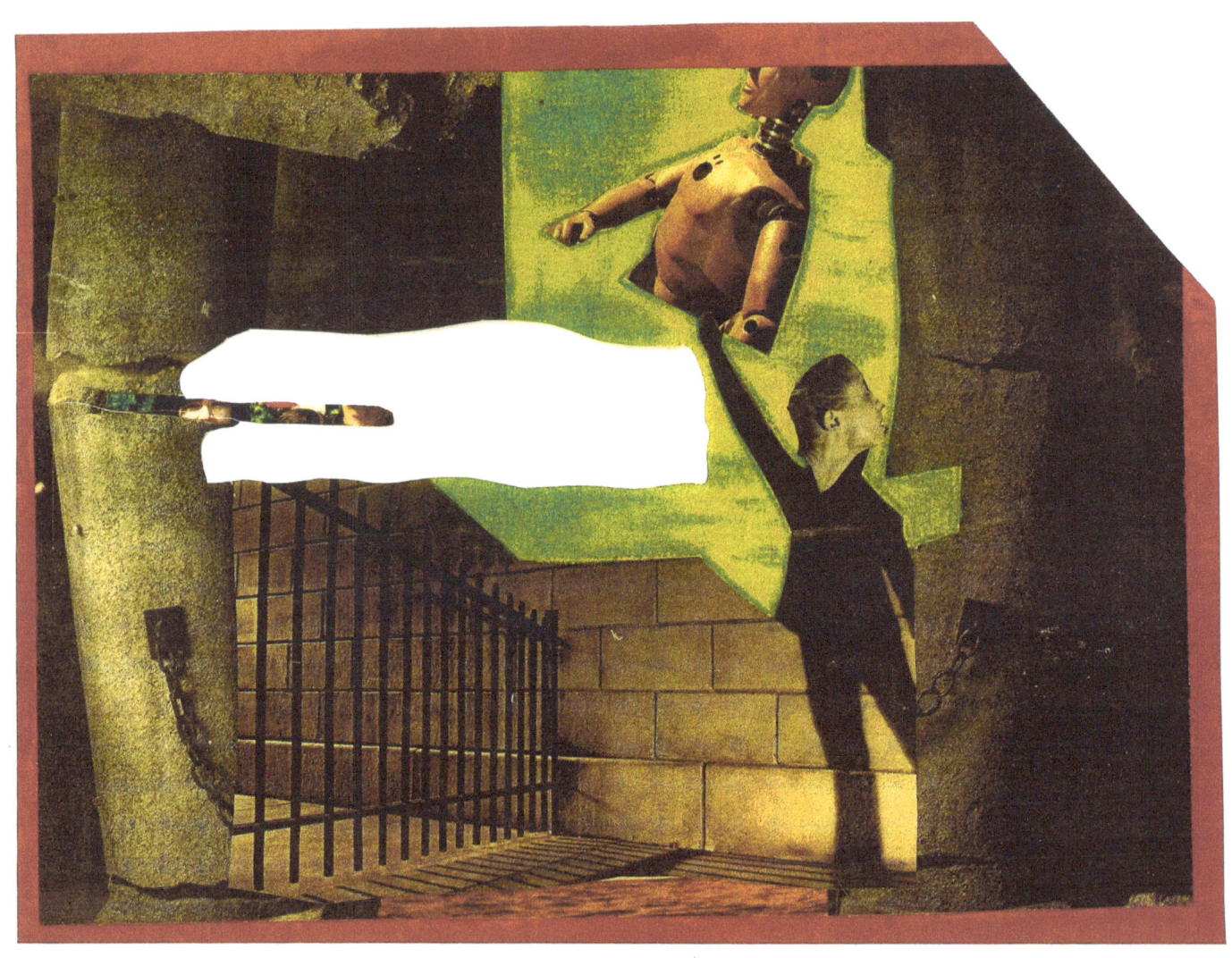

Family Ties

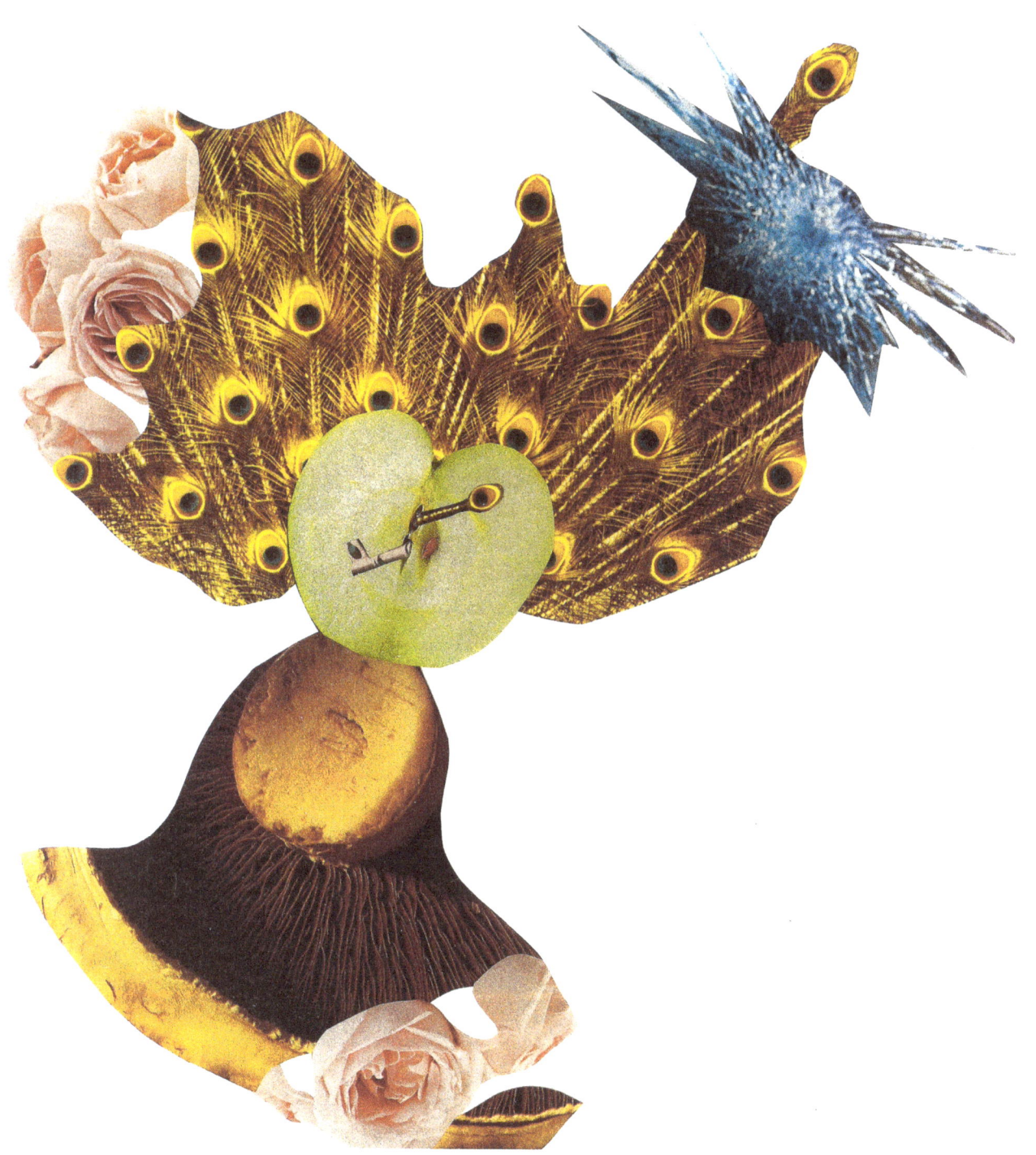

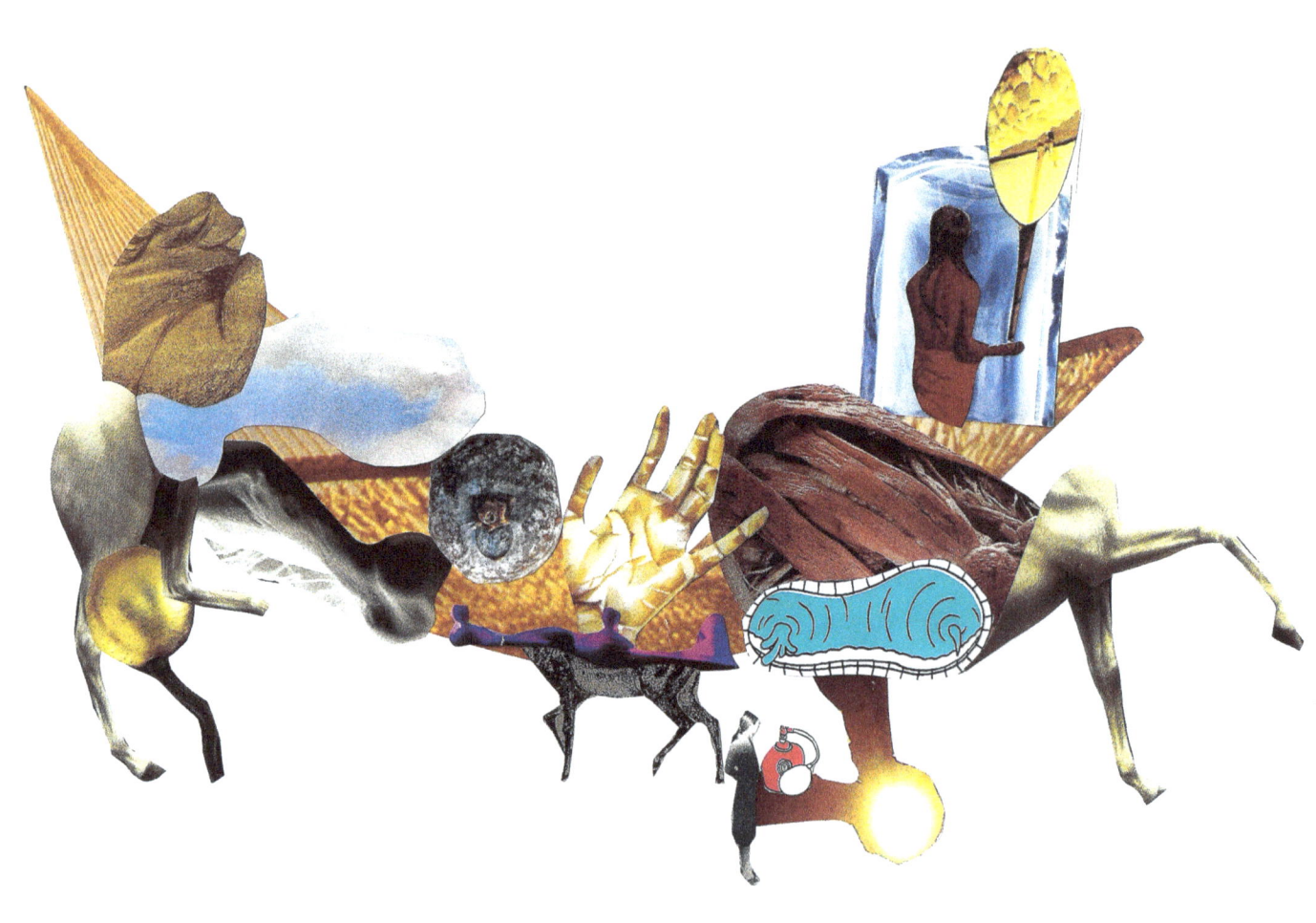

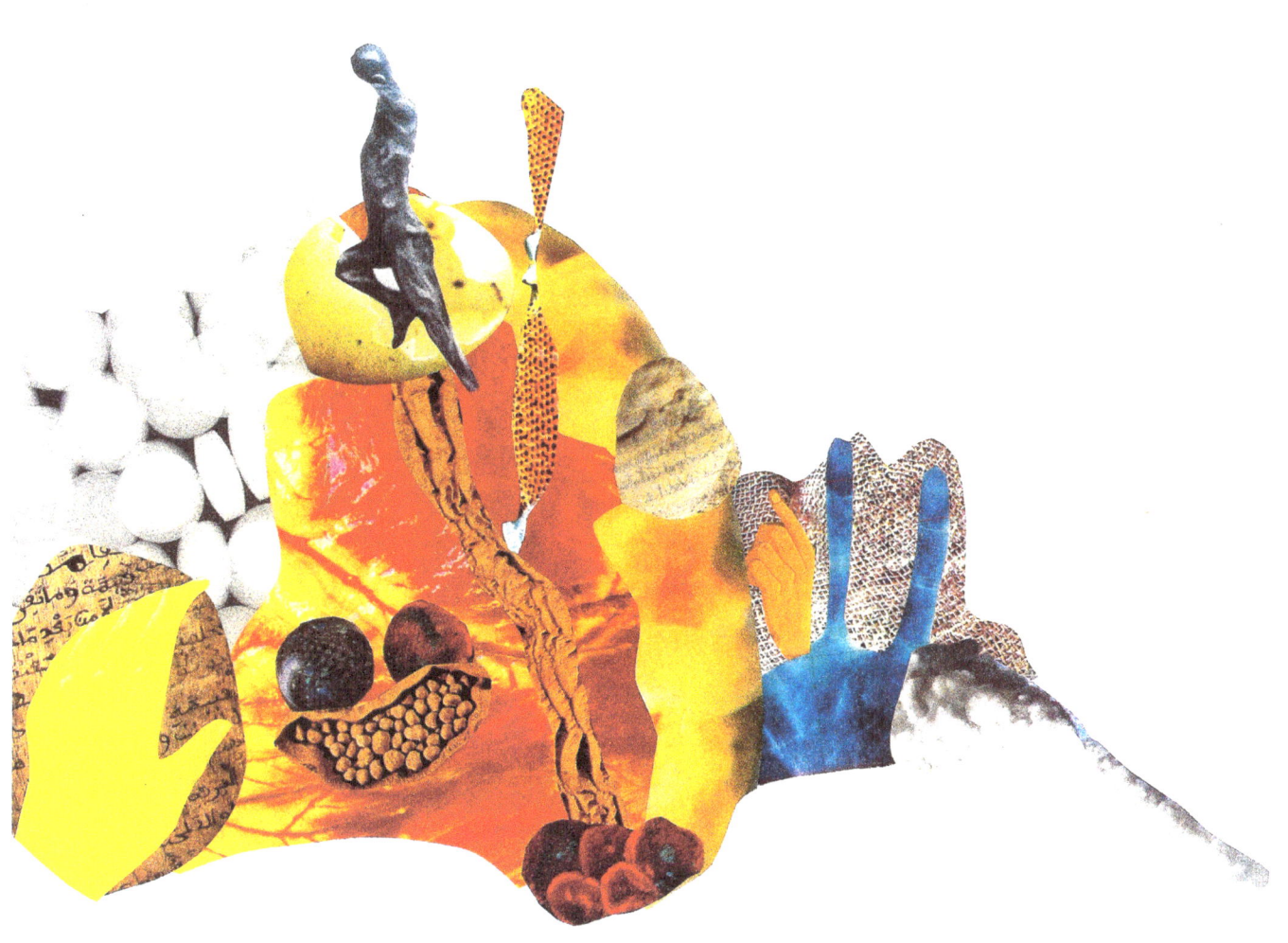

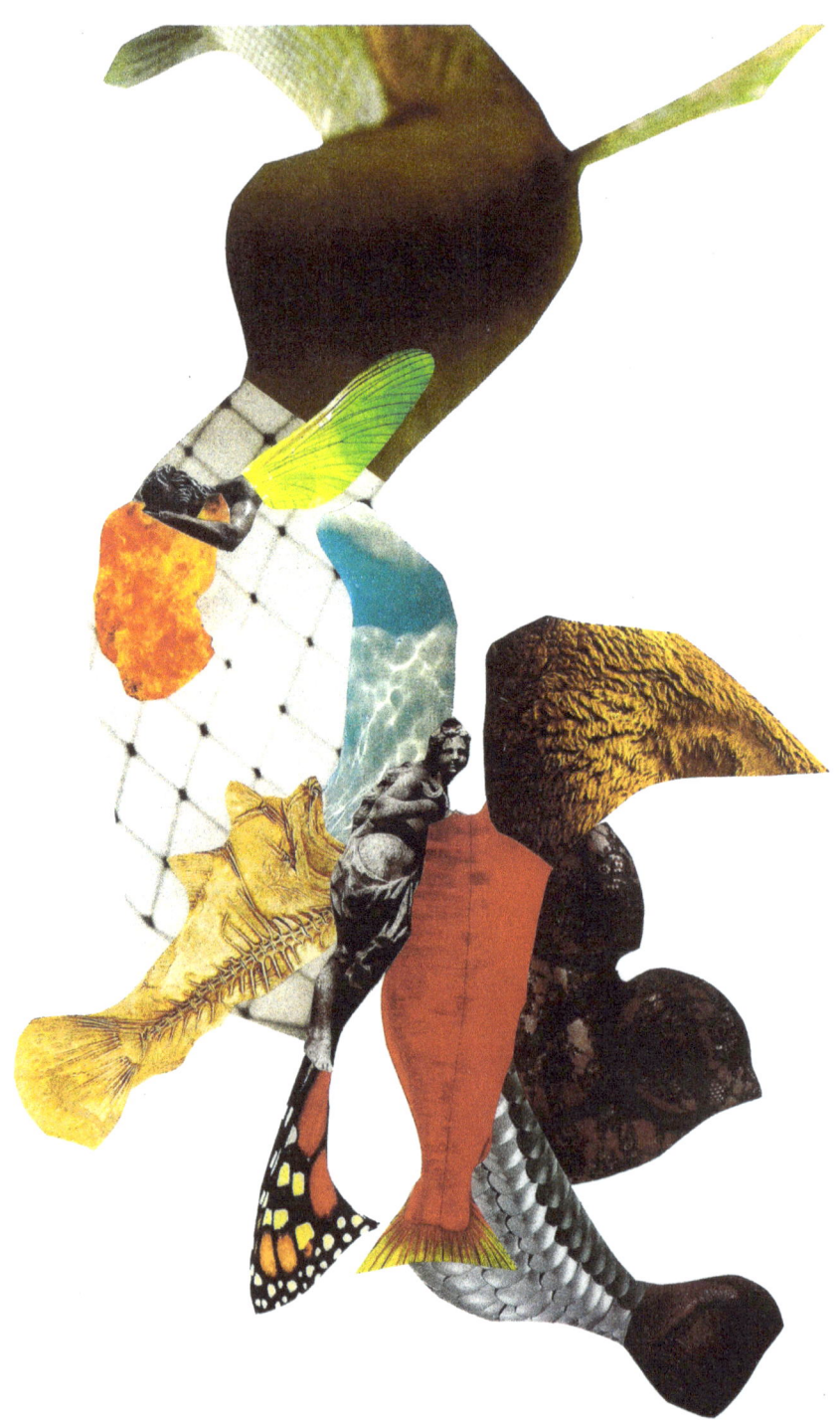

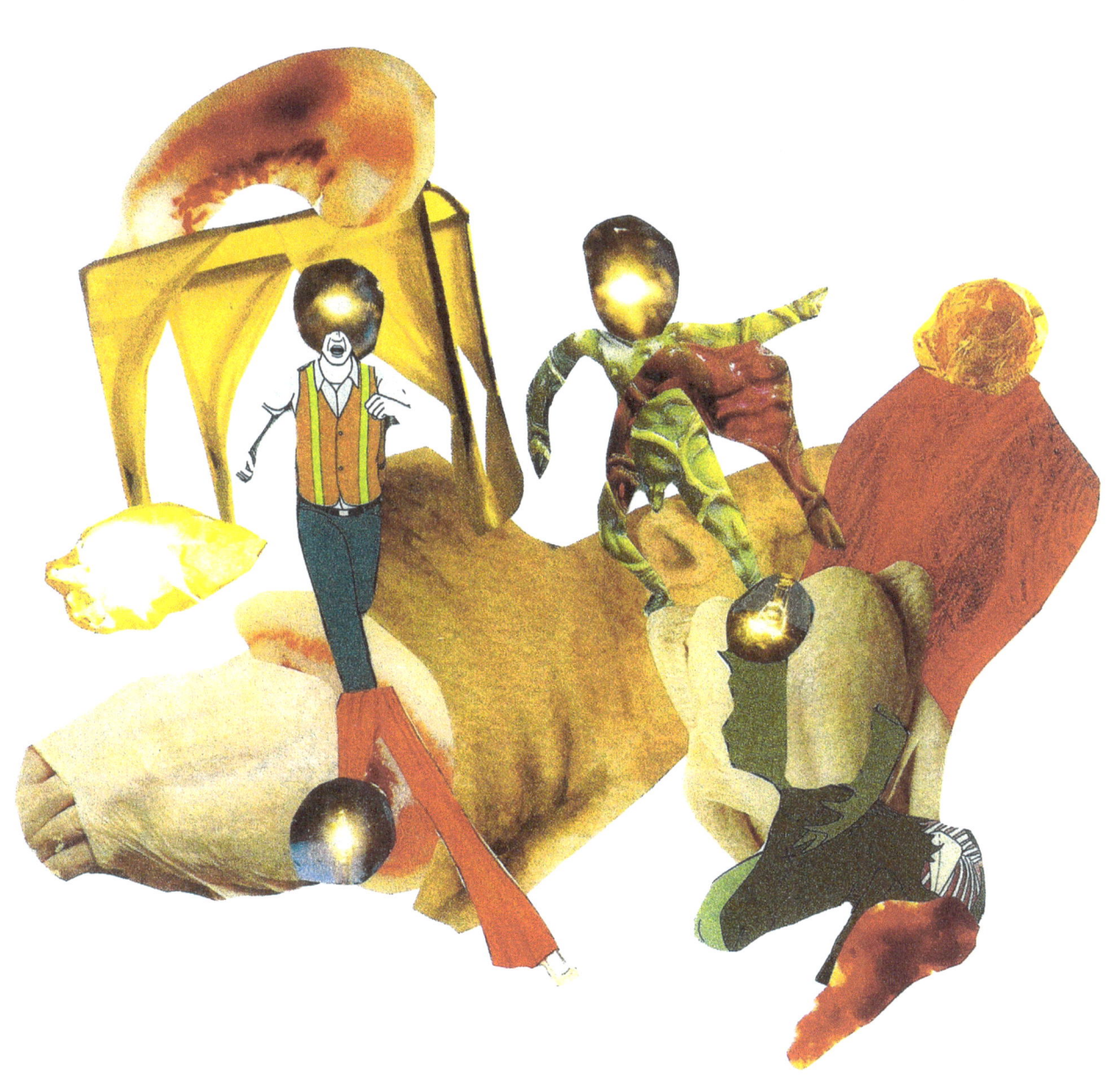

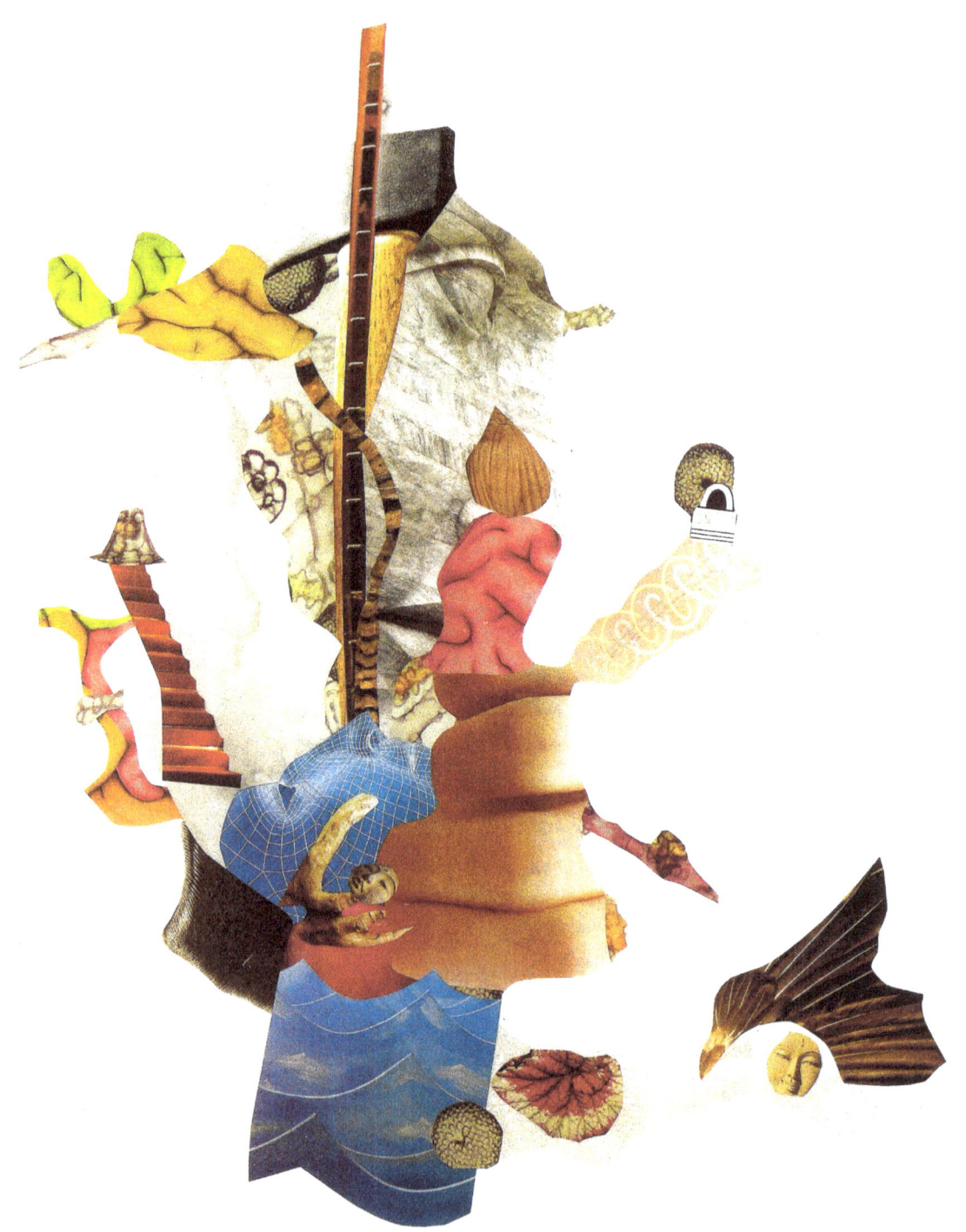

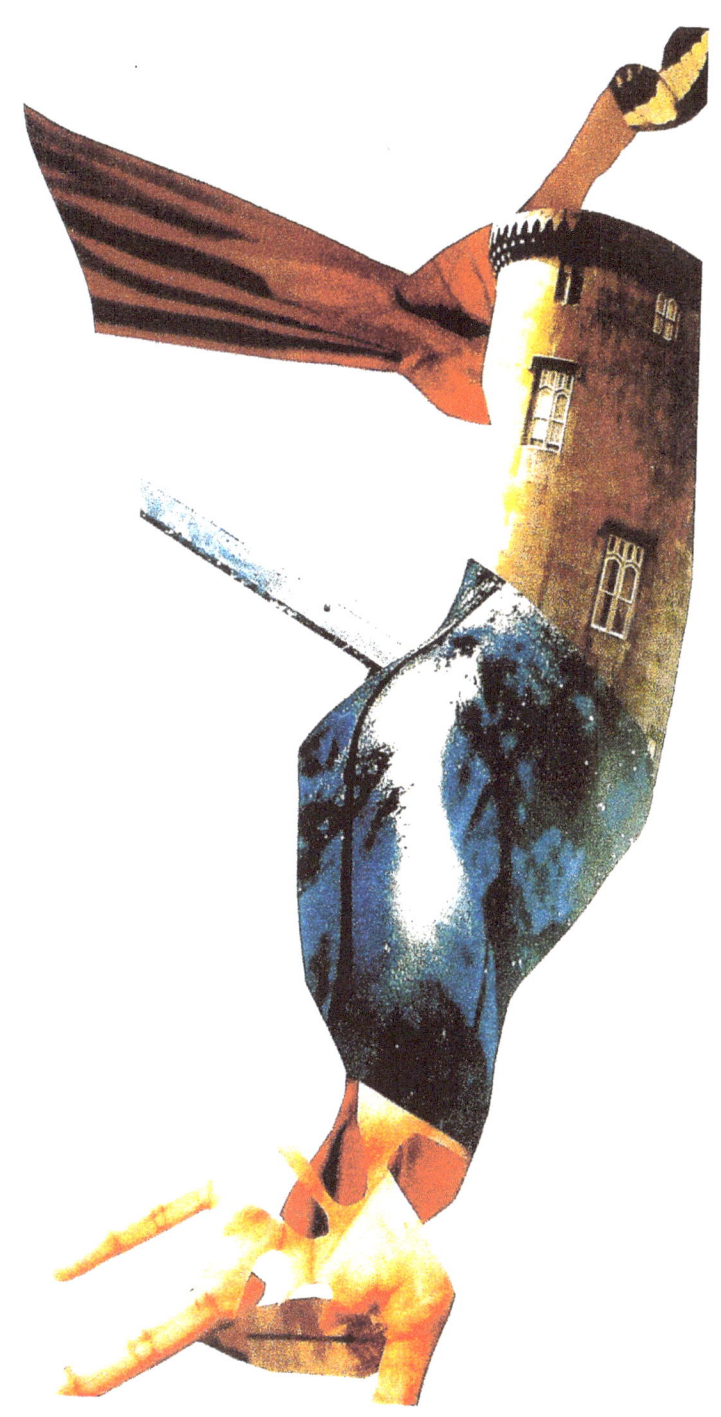

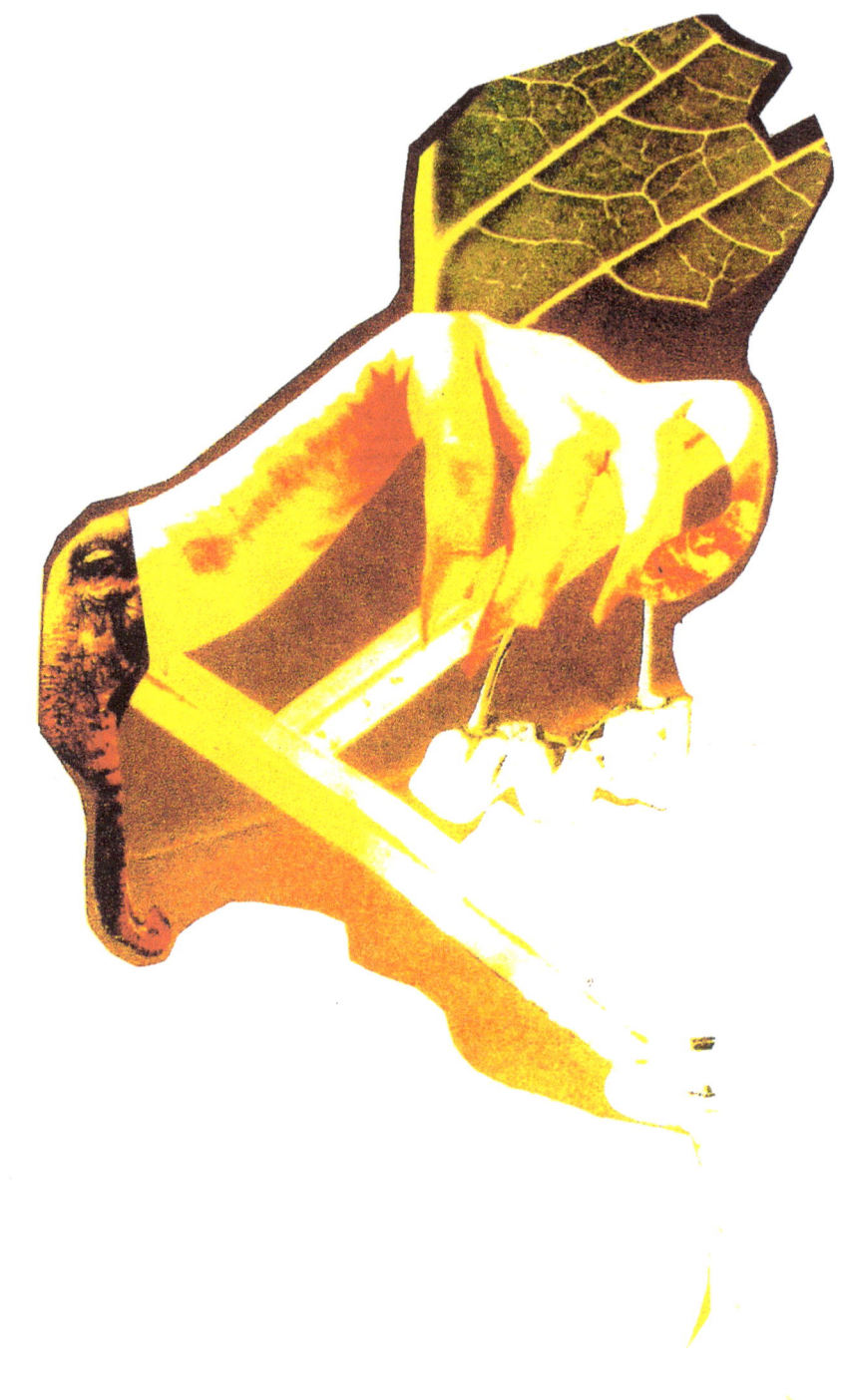

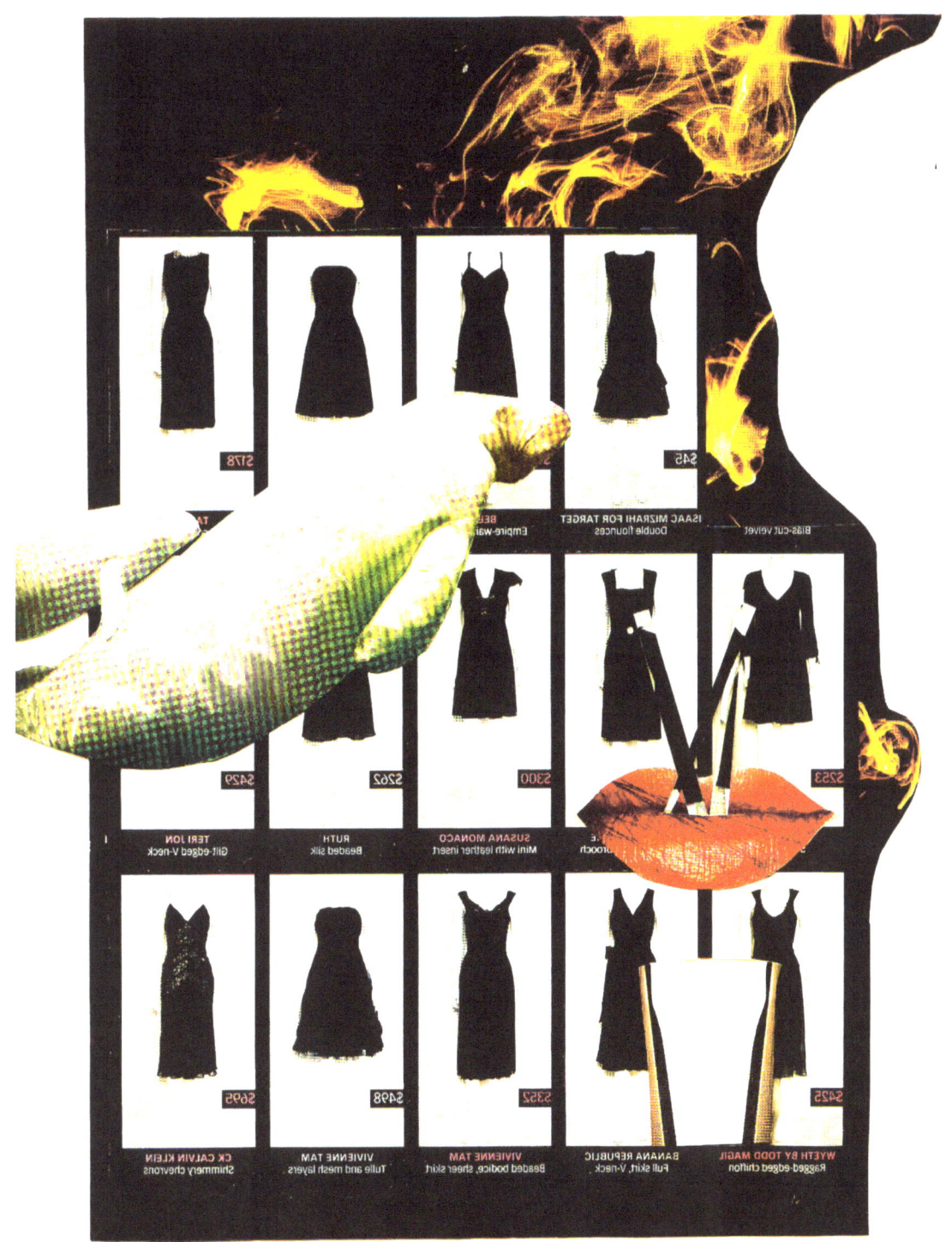

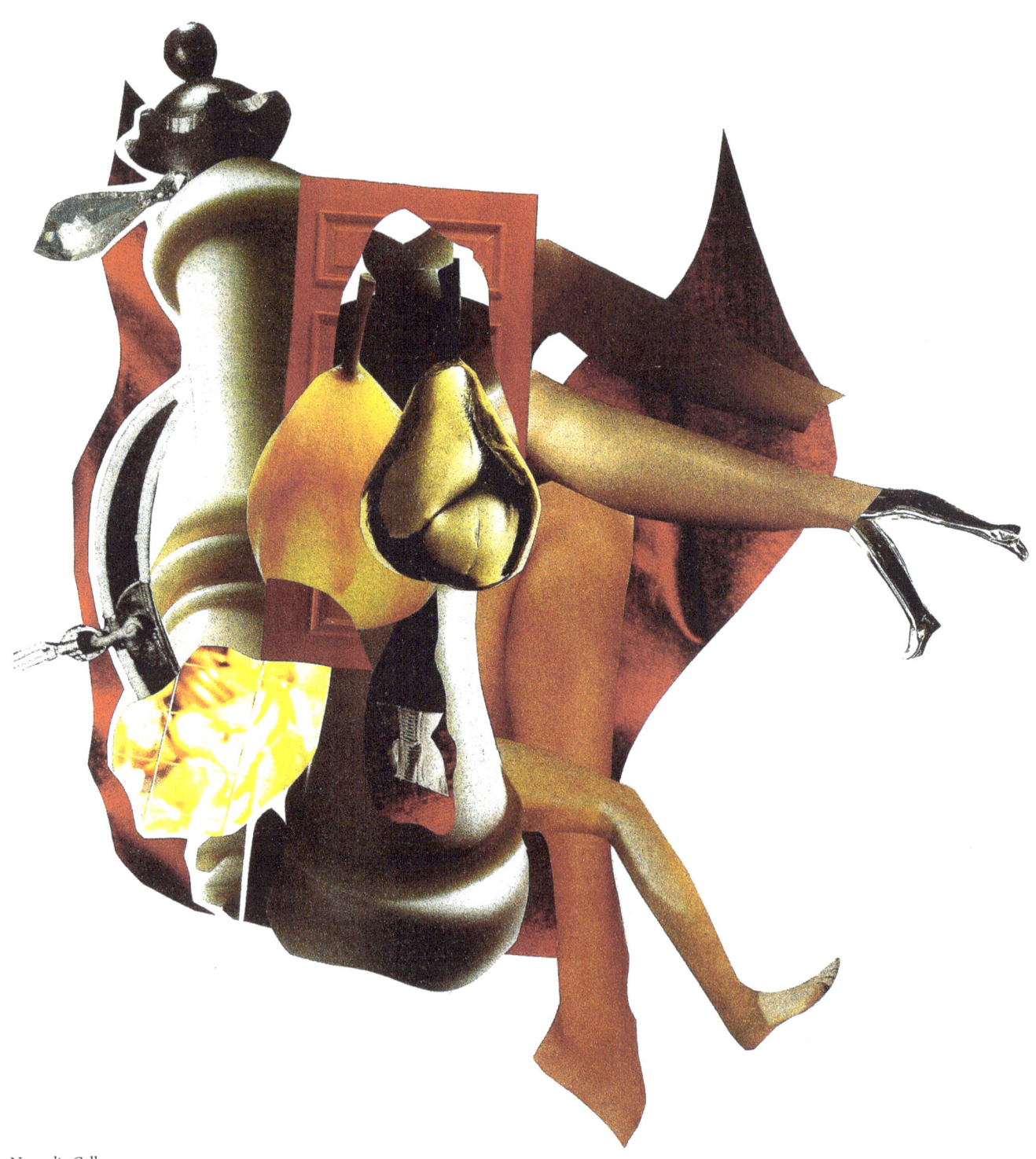

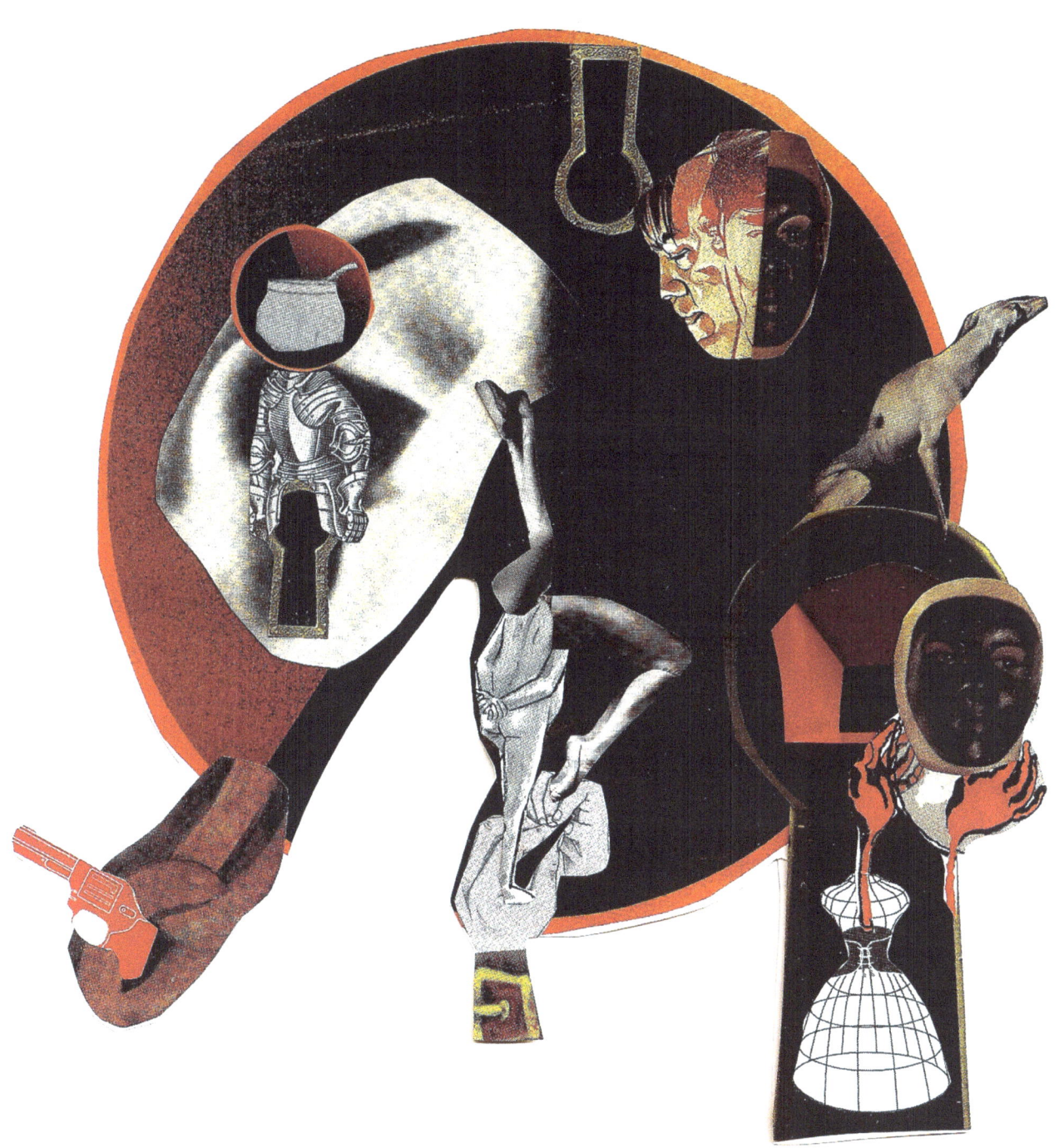

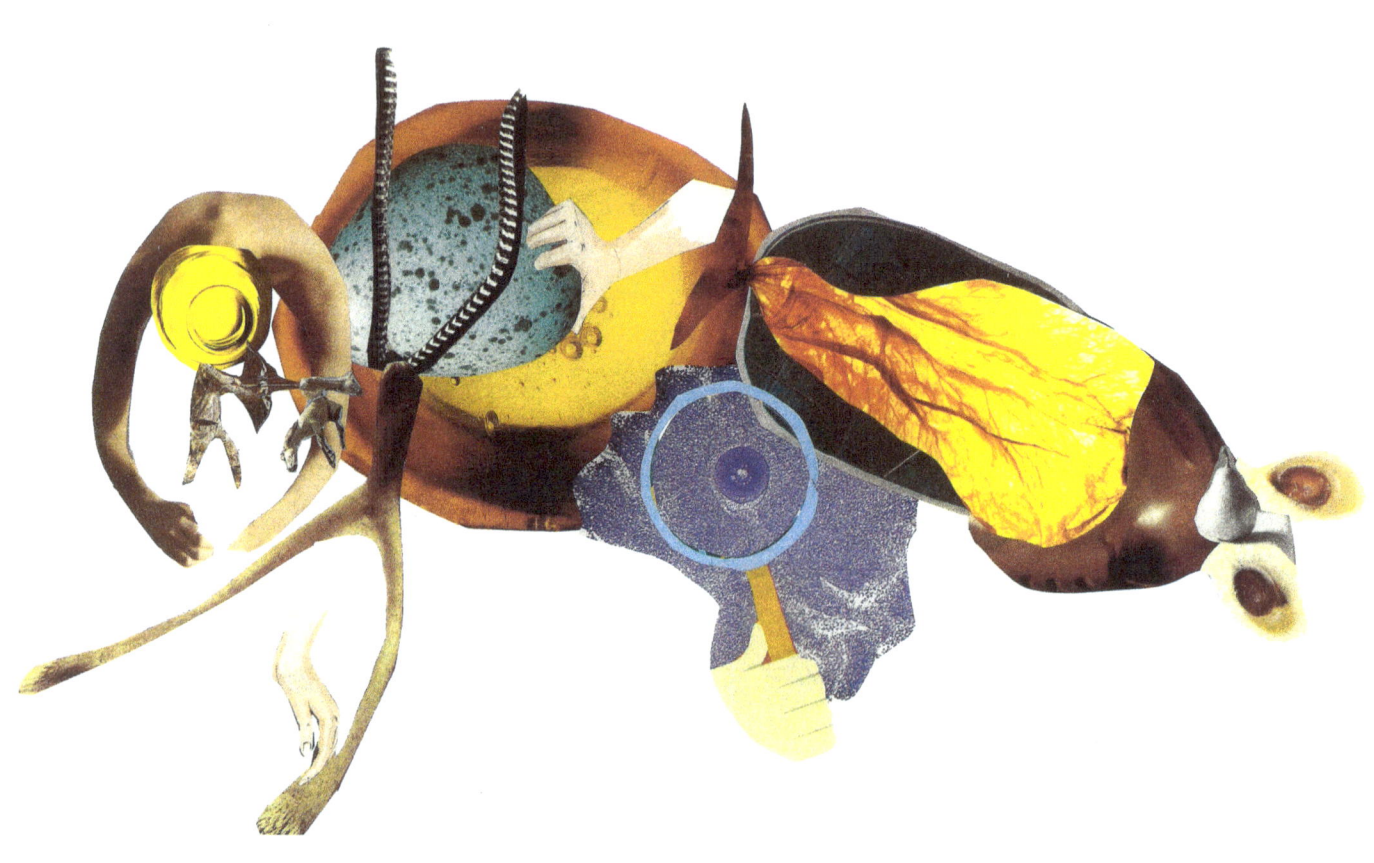

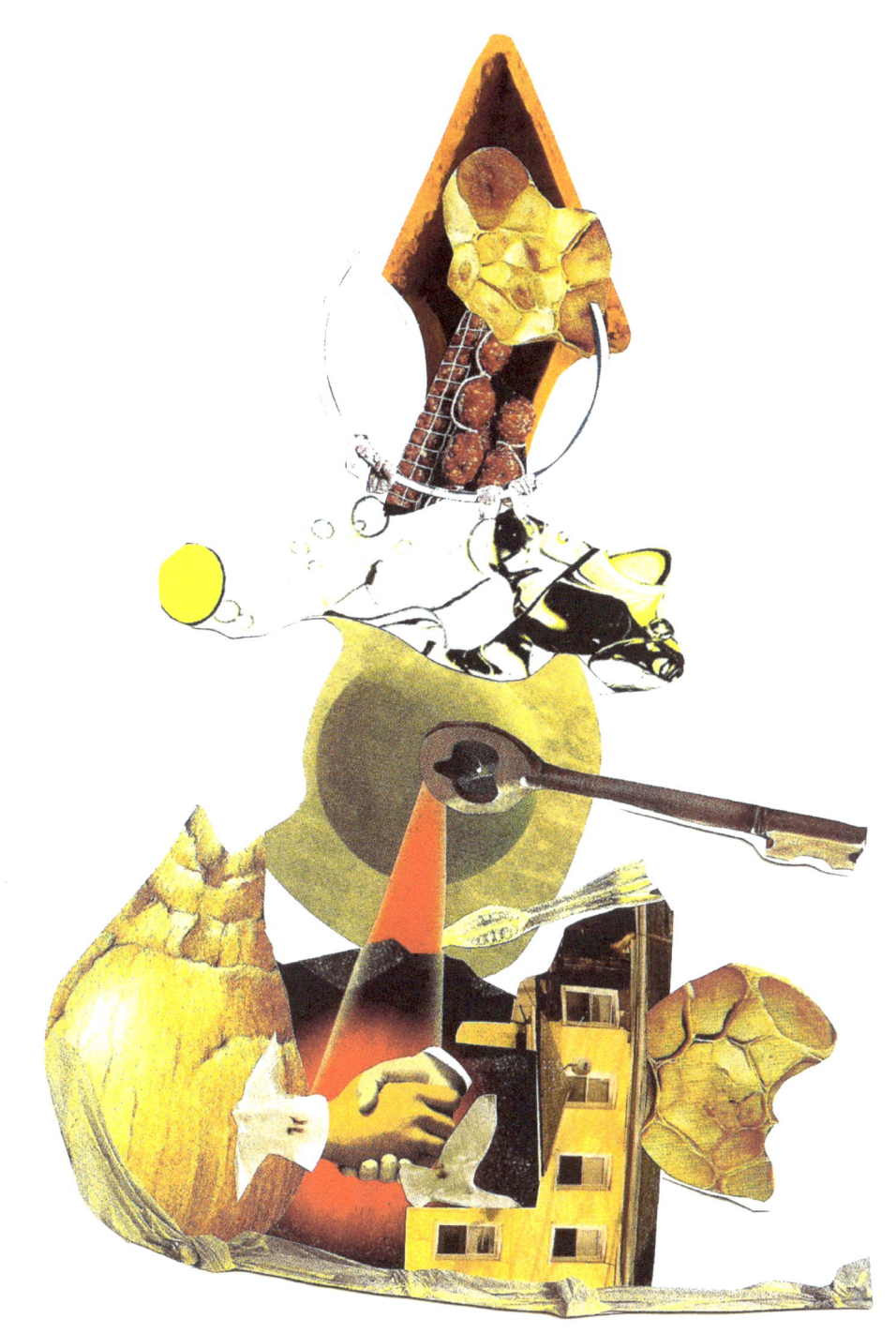

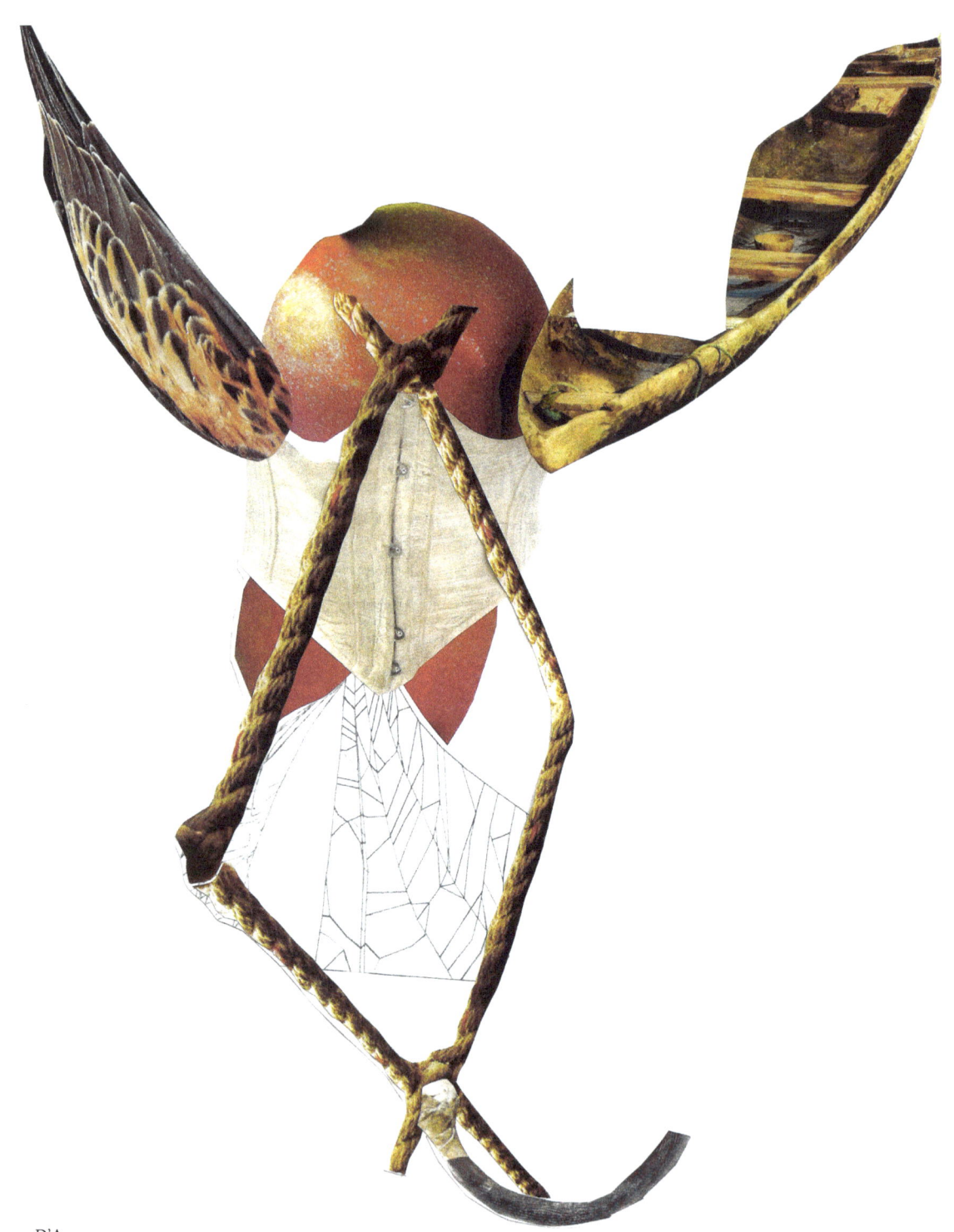

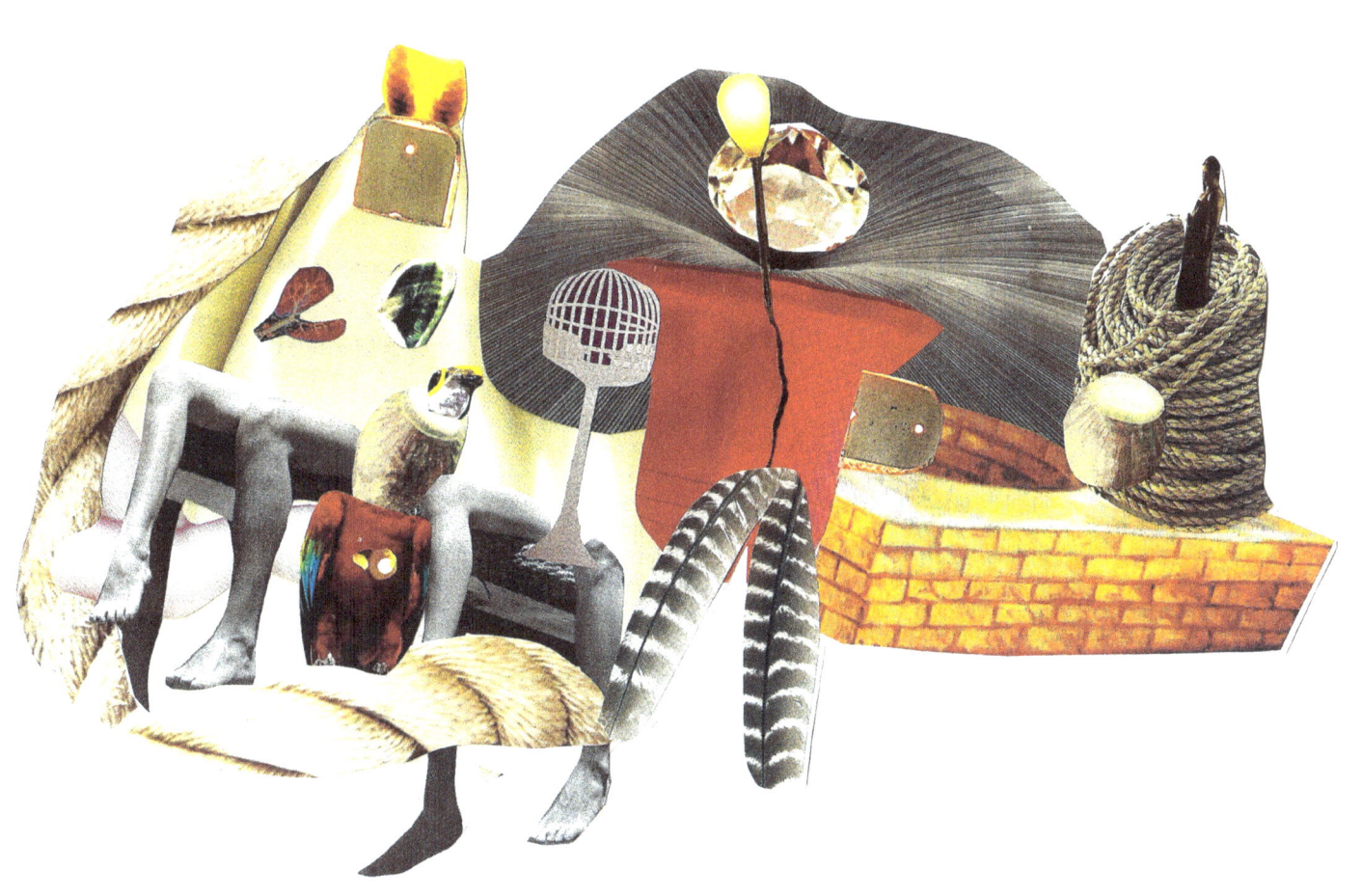

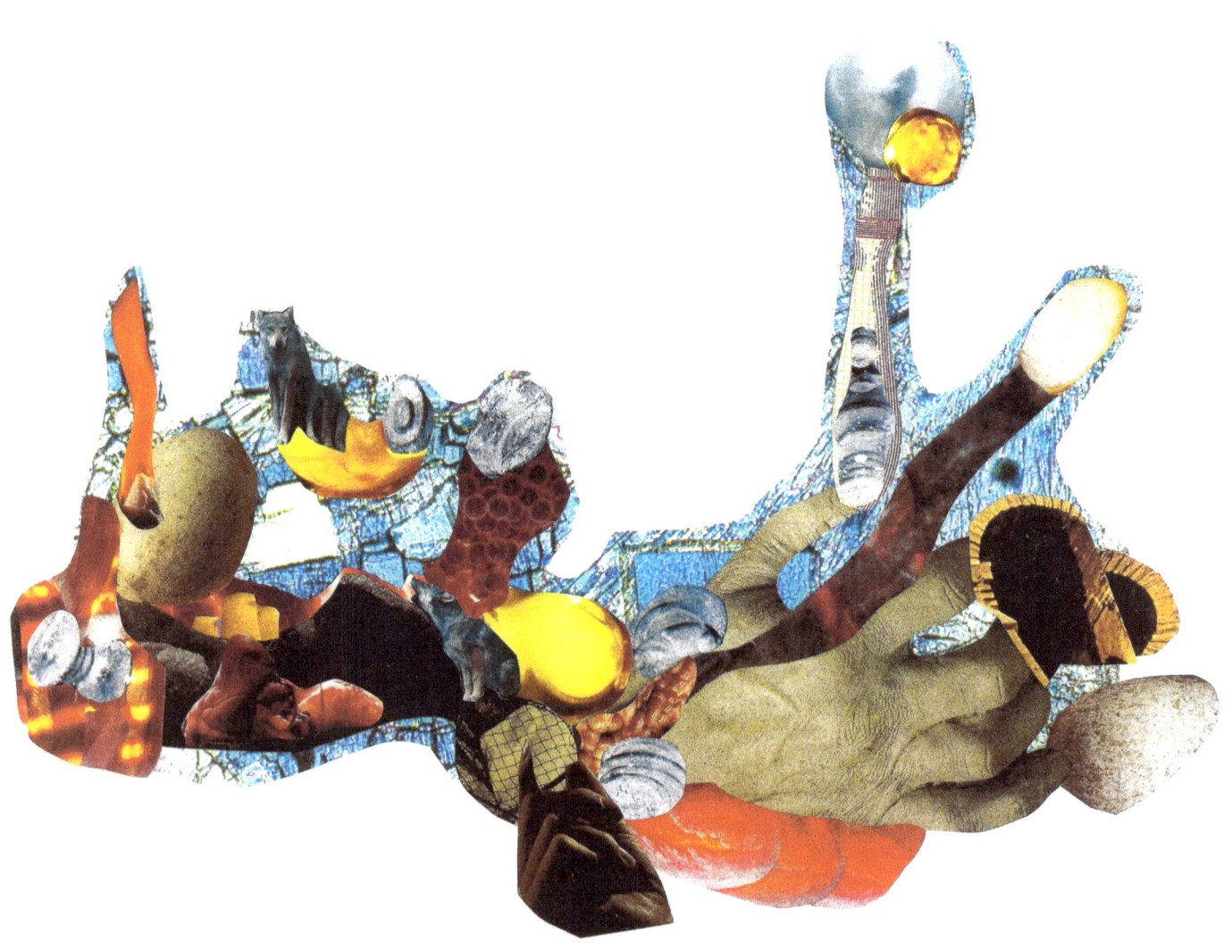

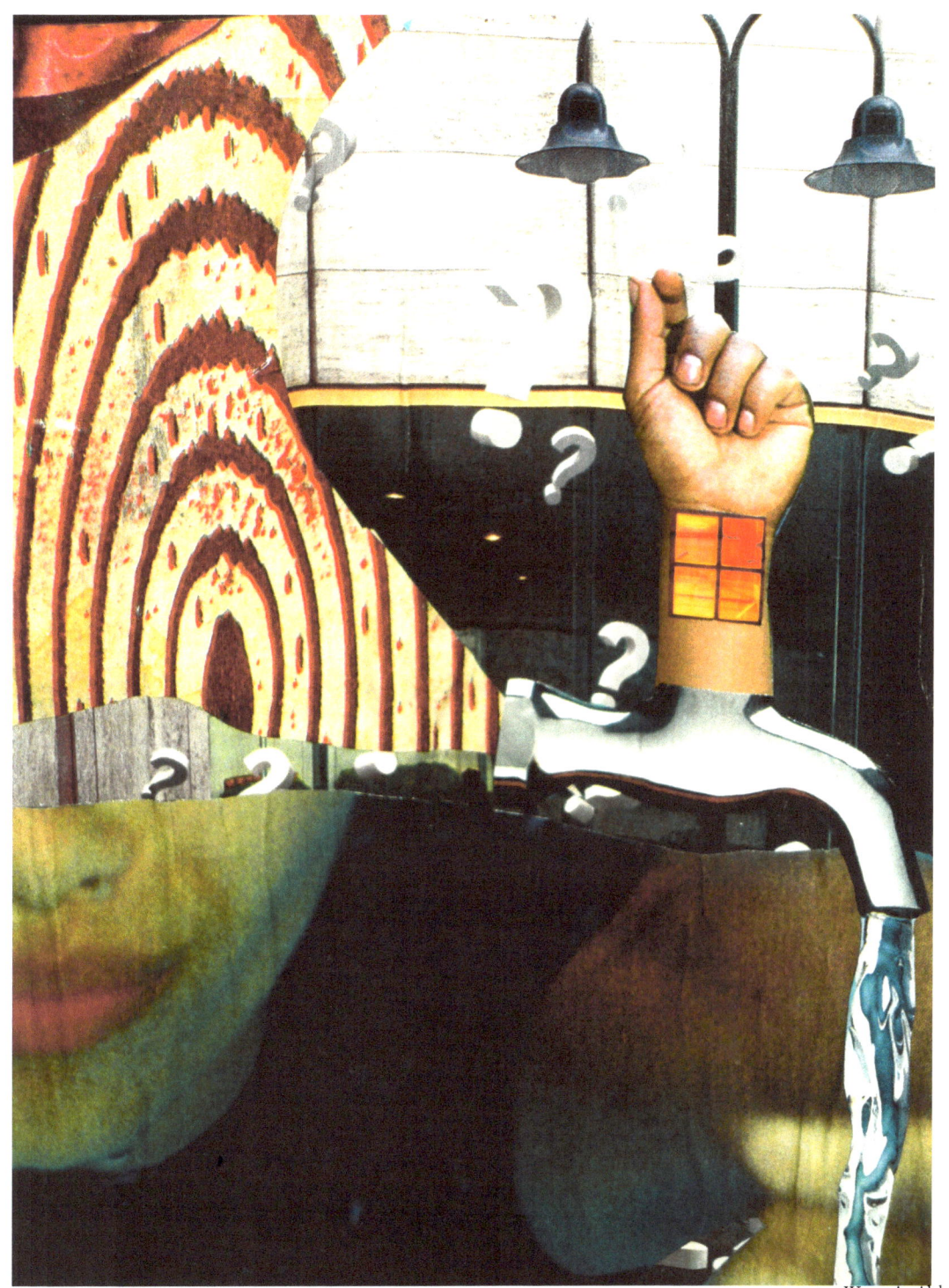

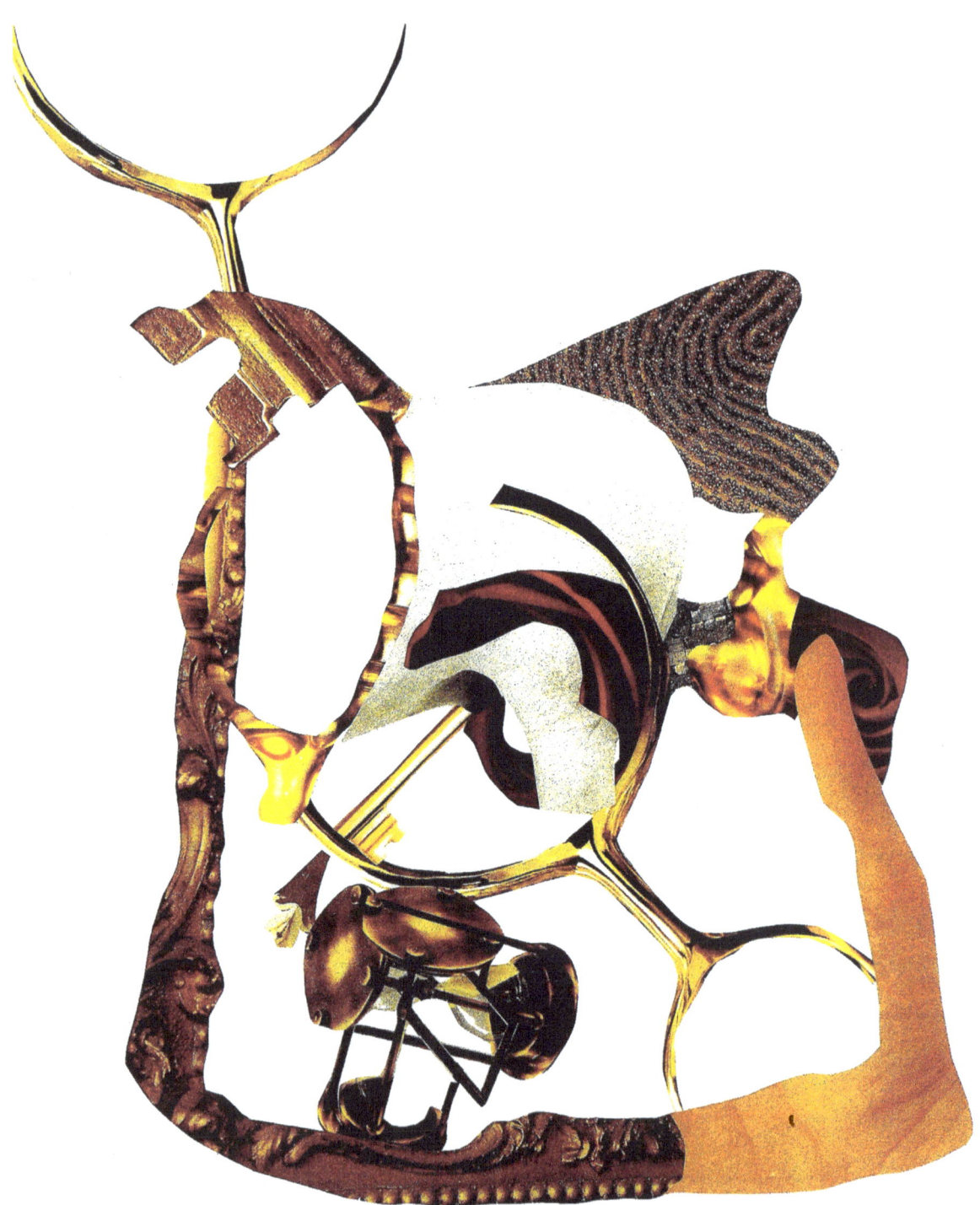

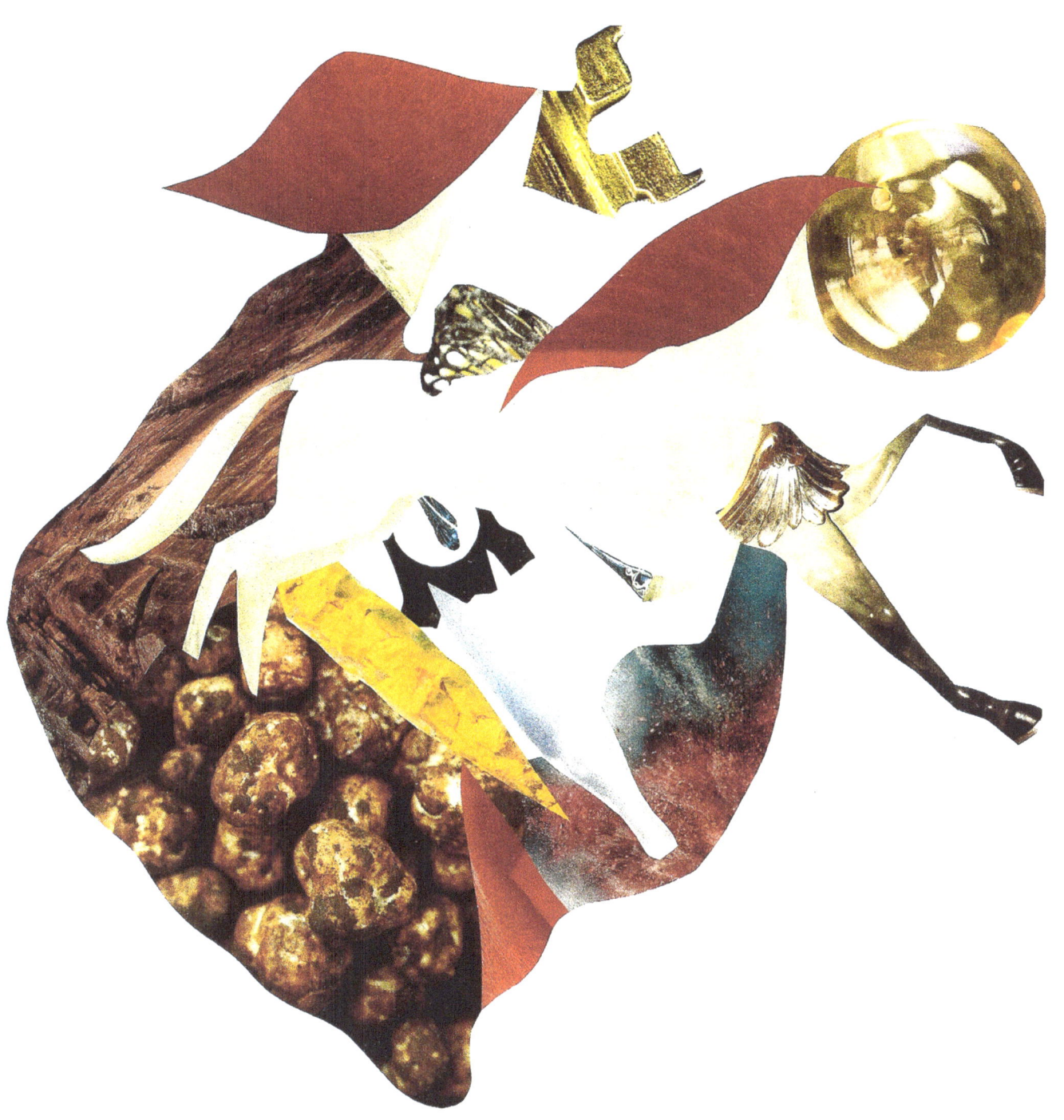

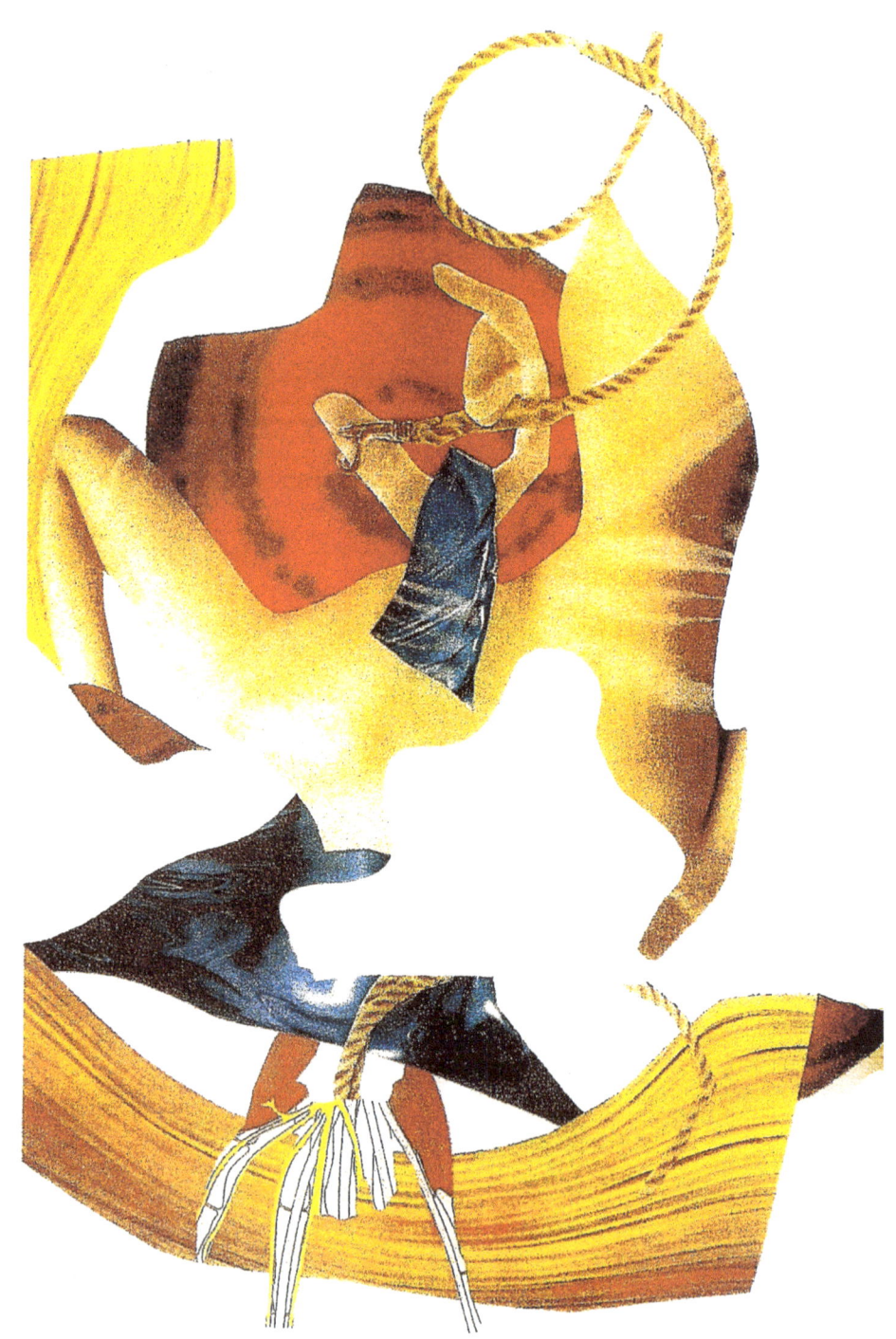

Cyborg chant

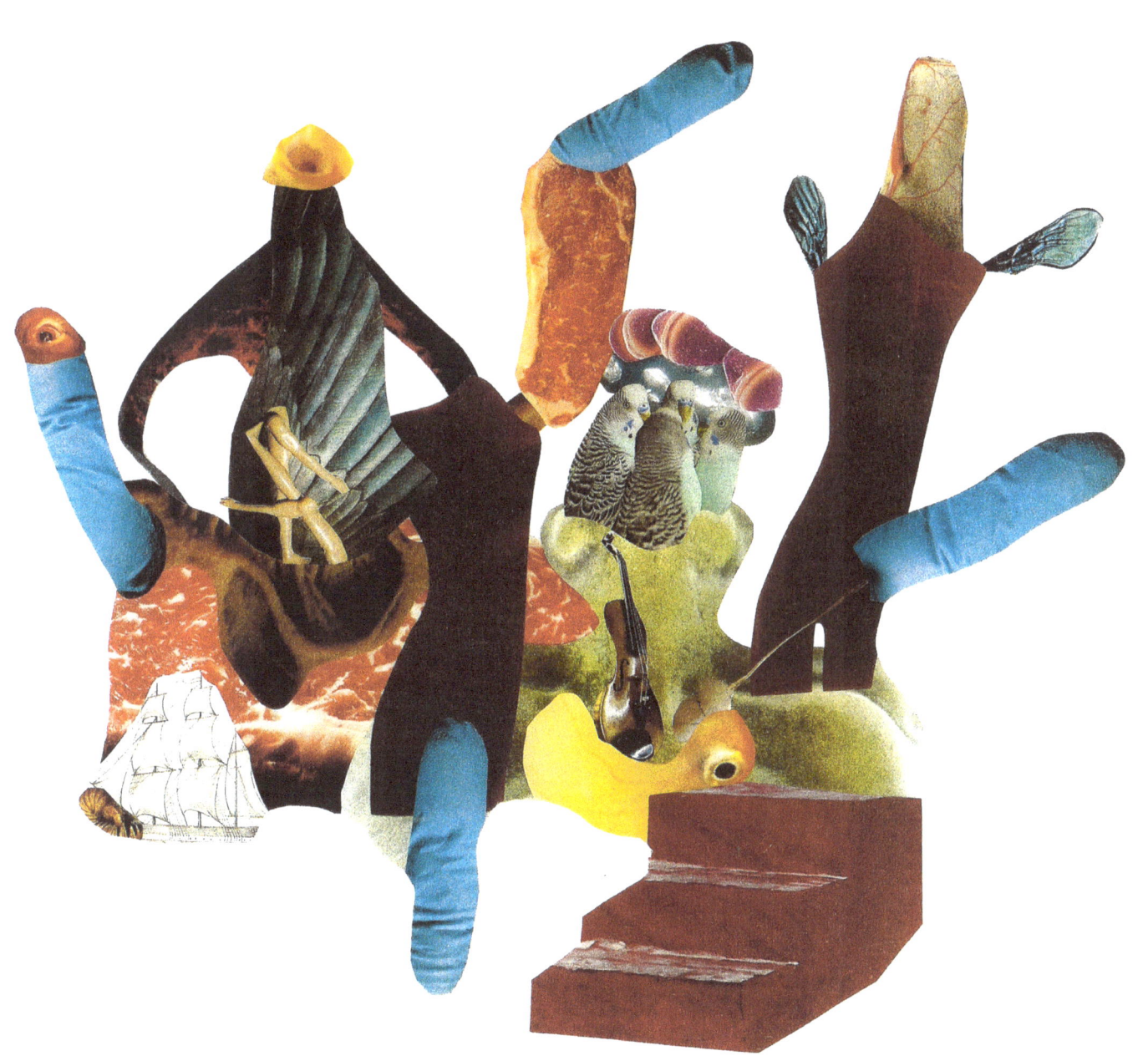

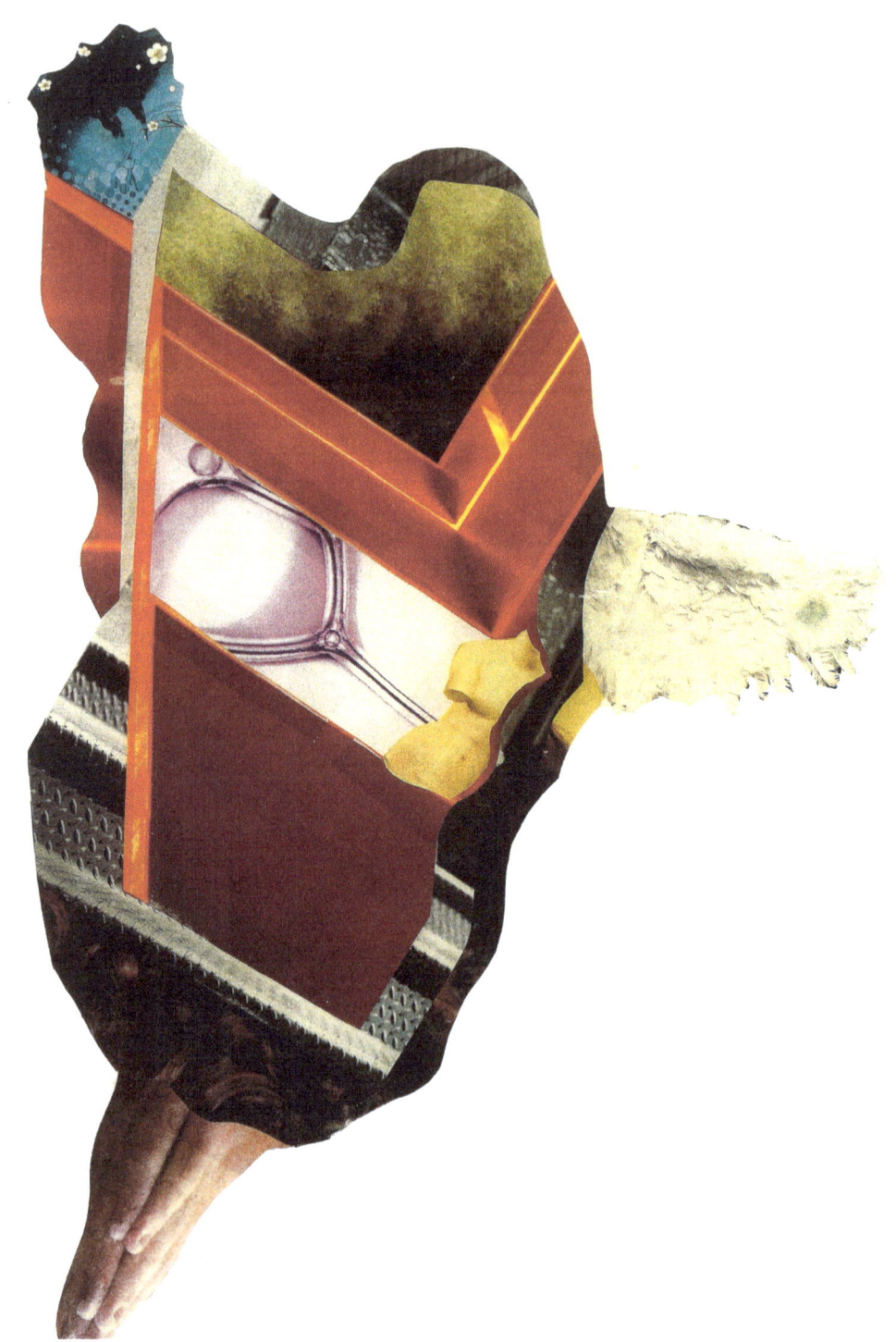

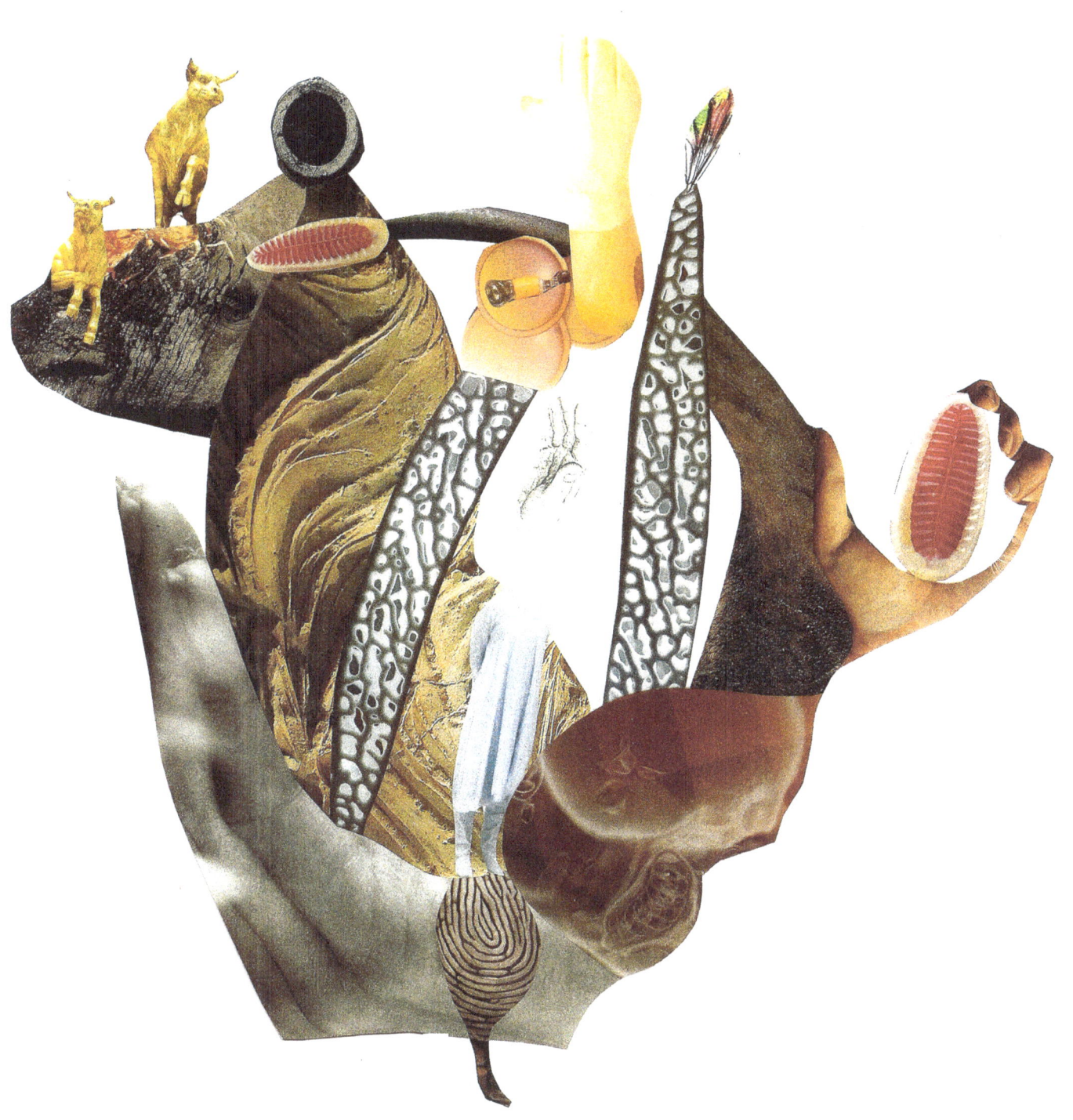

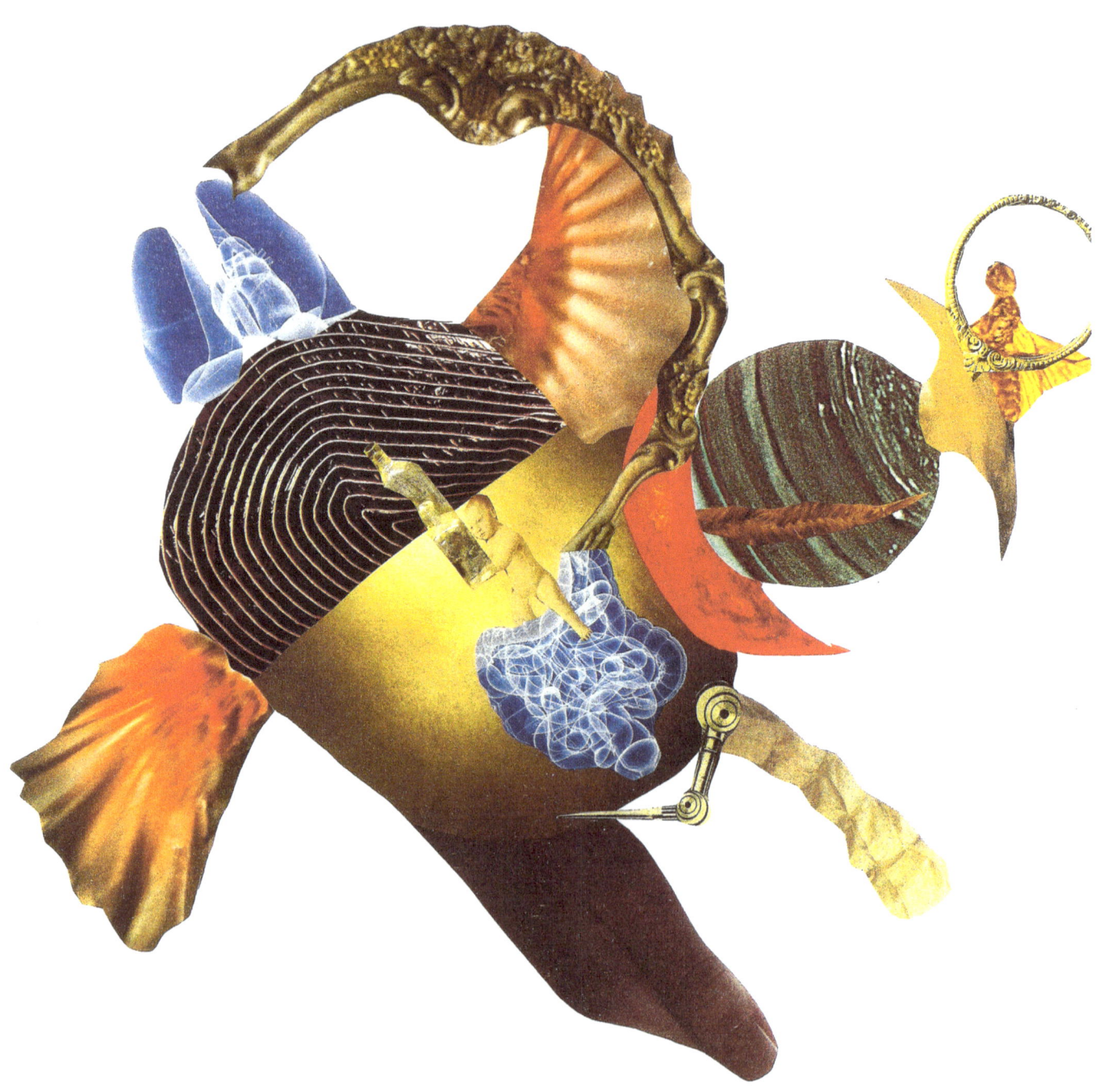

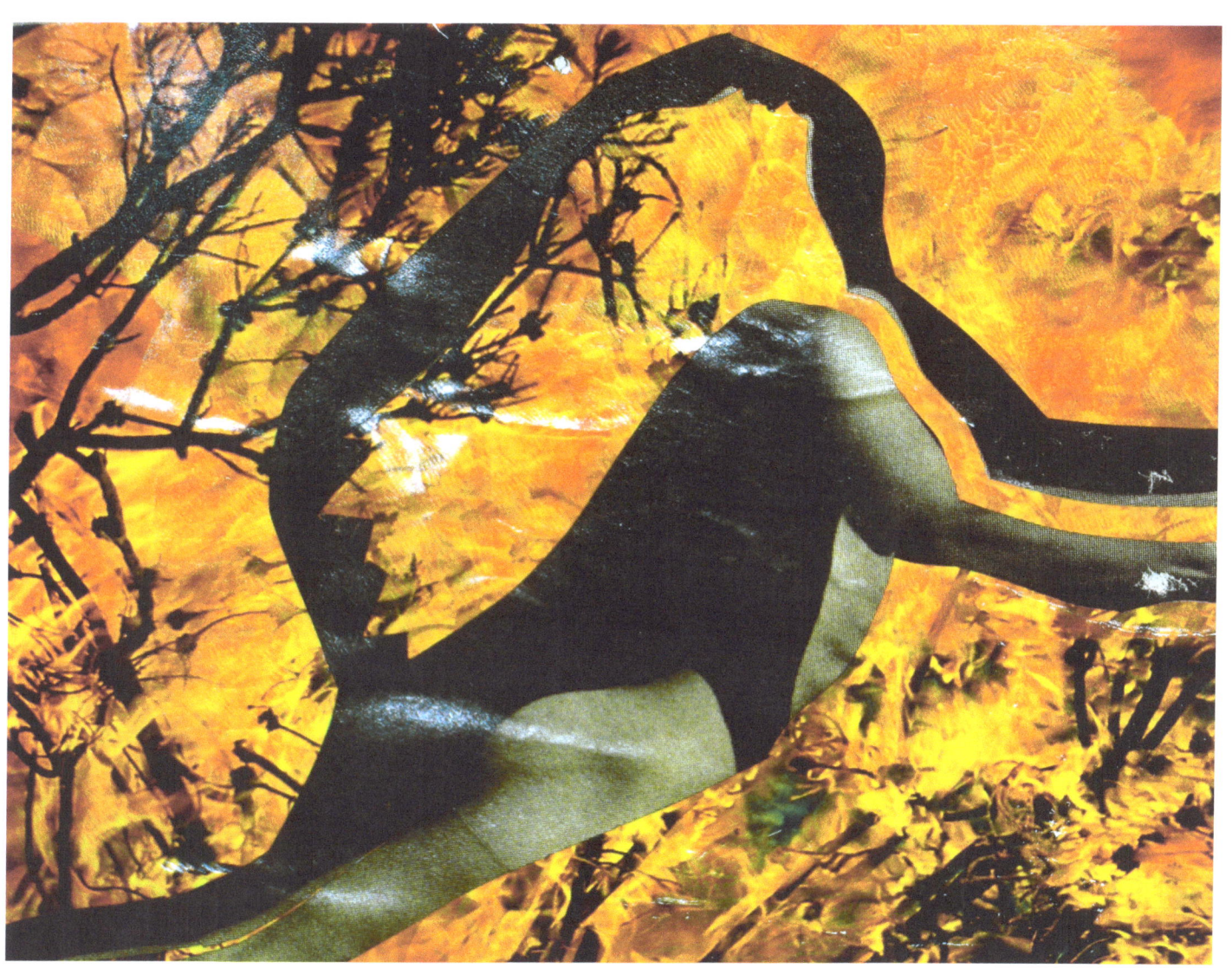

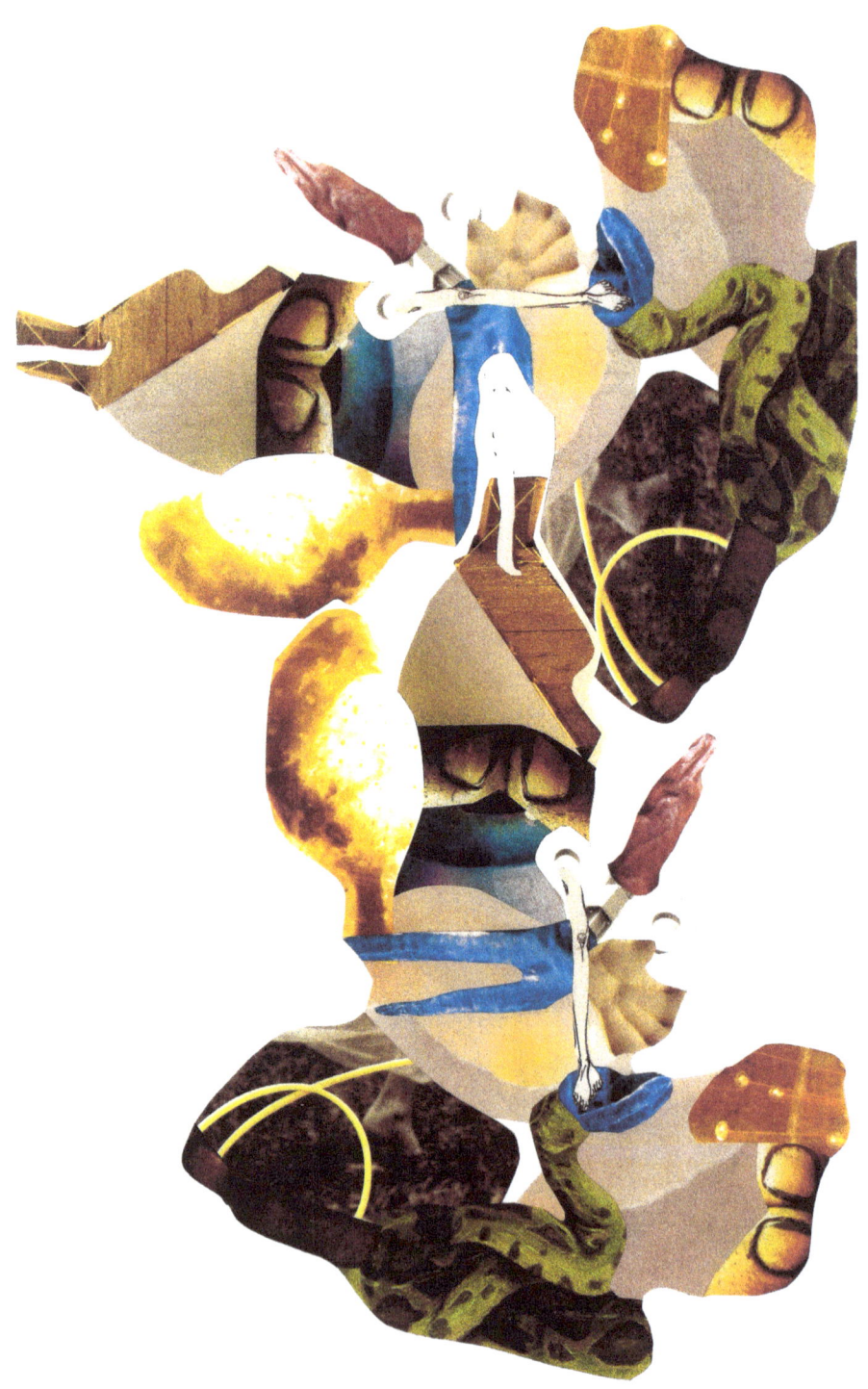

Serpent We

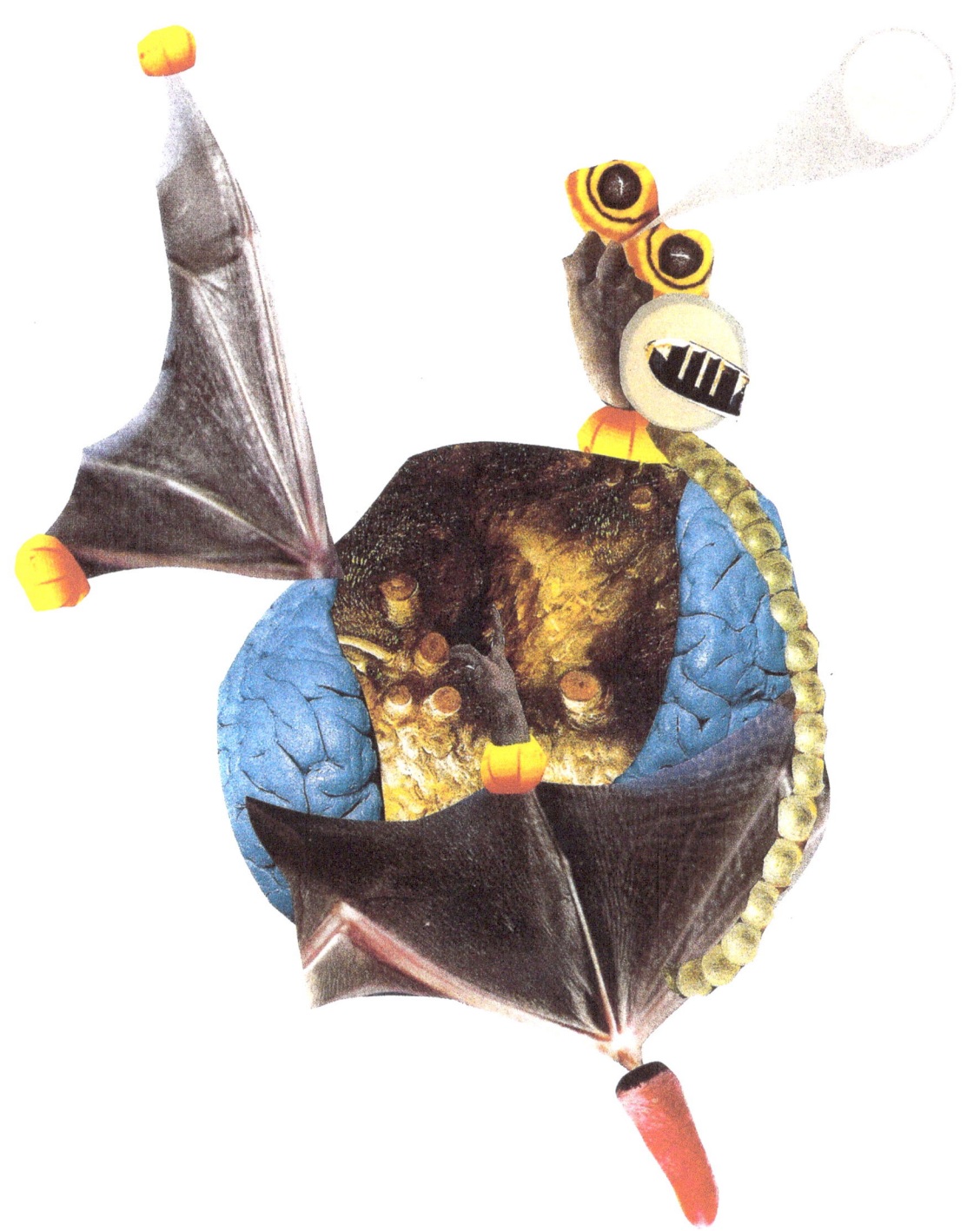

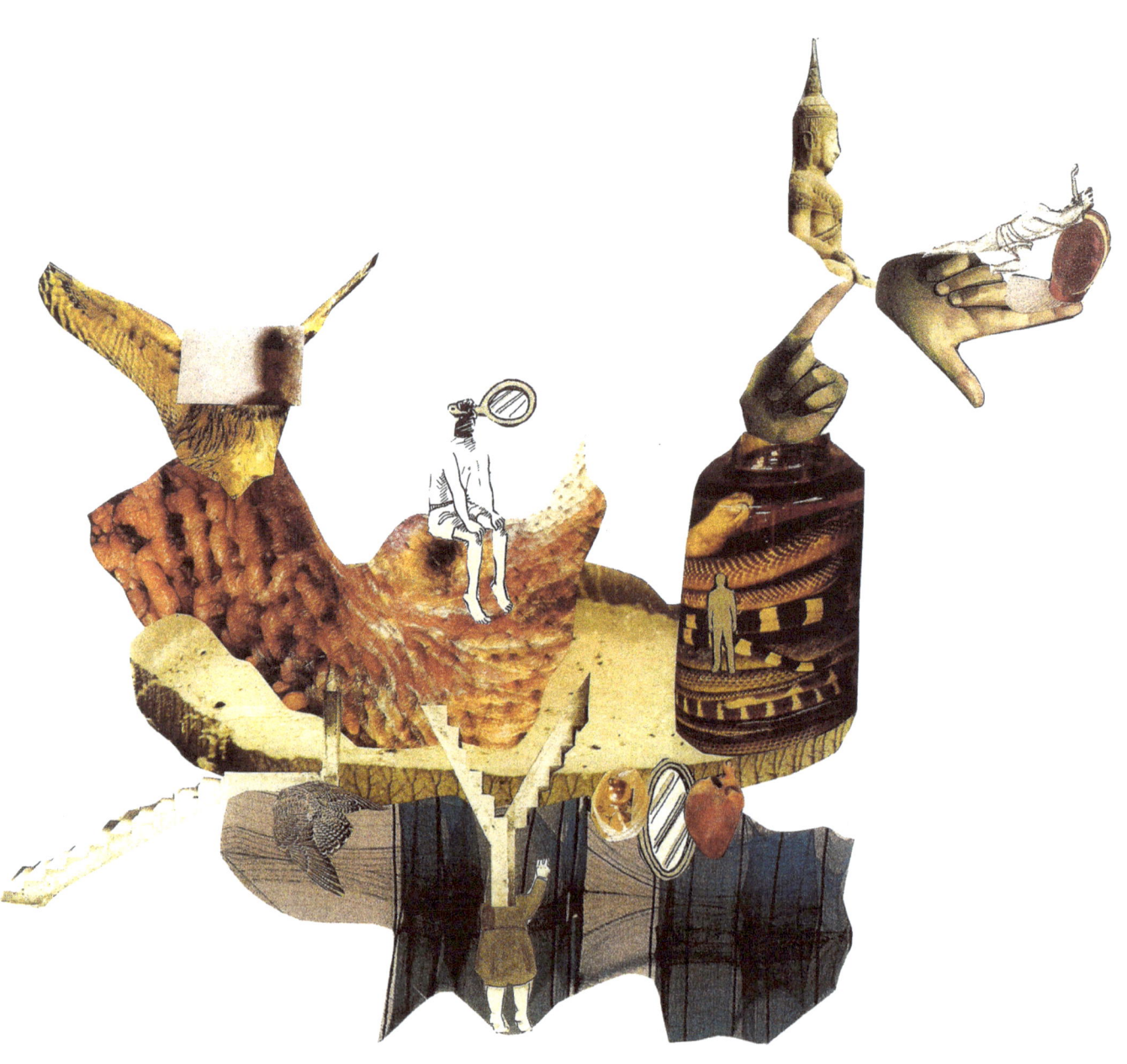

A City's Vista Is Viscera Of The Simultaneous Self

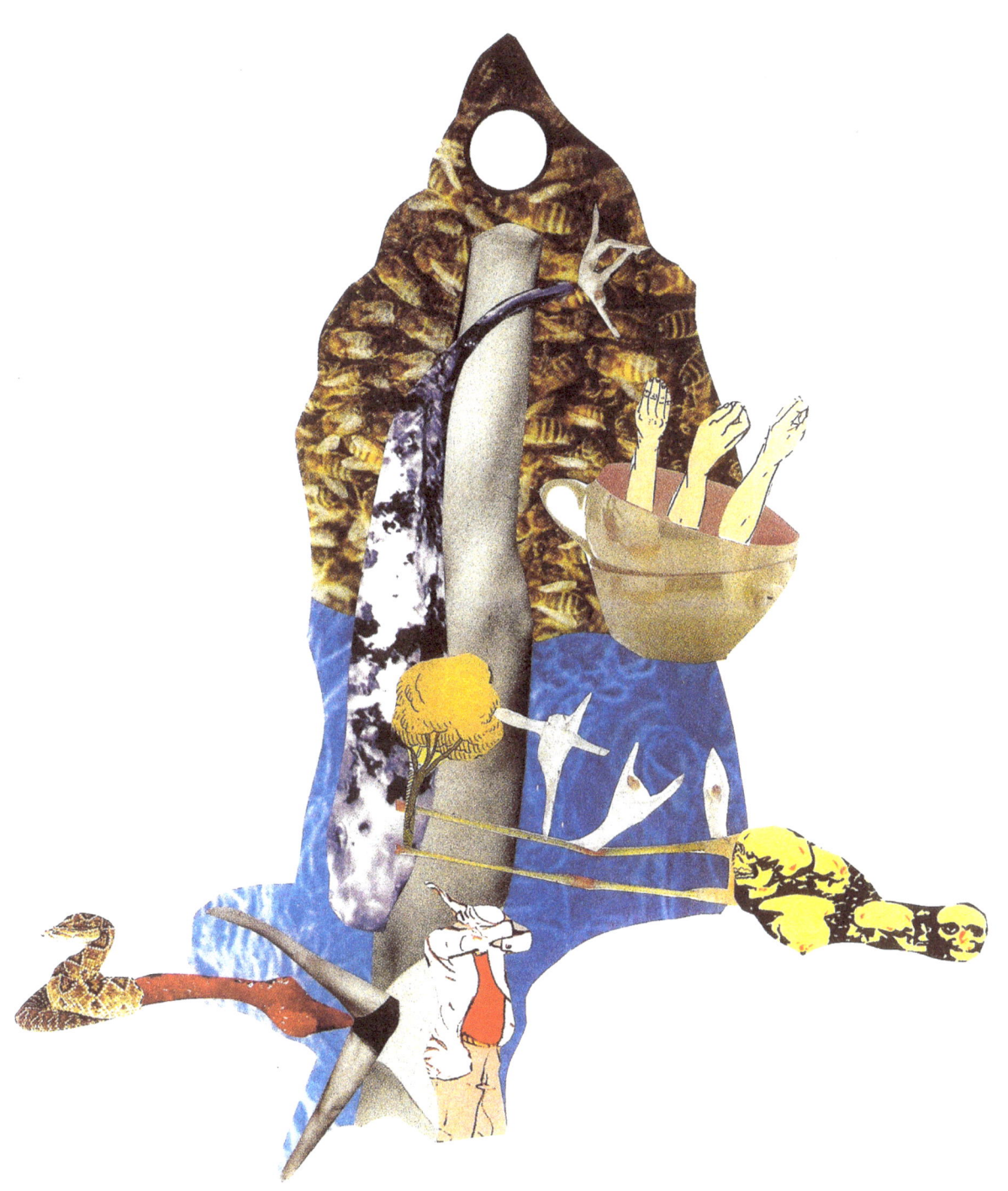

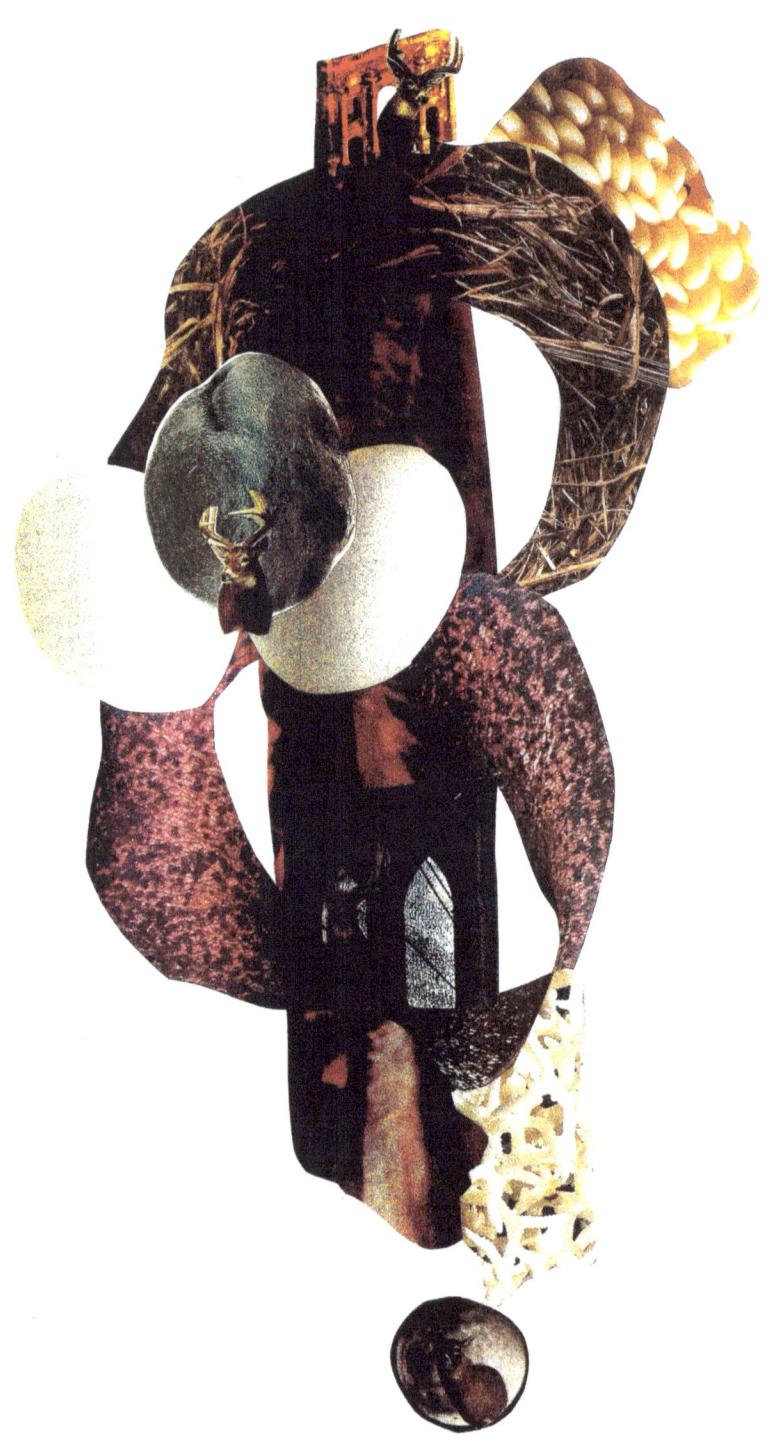

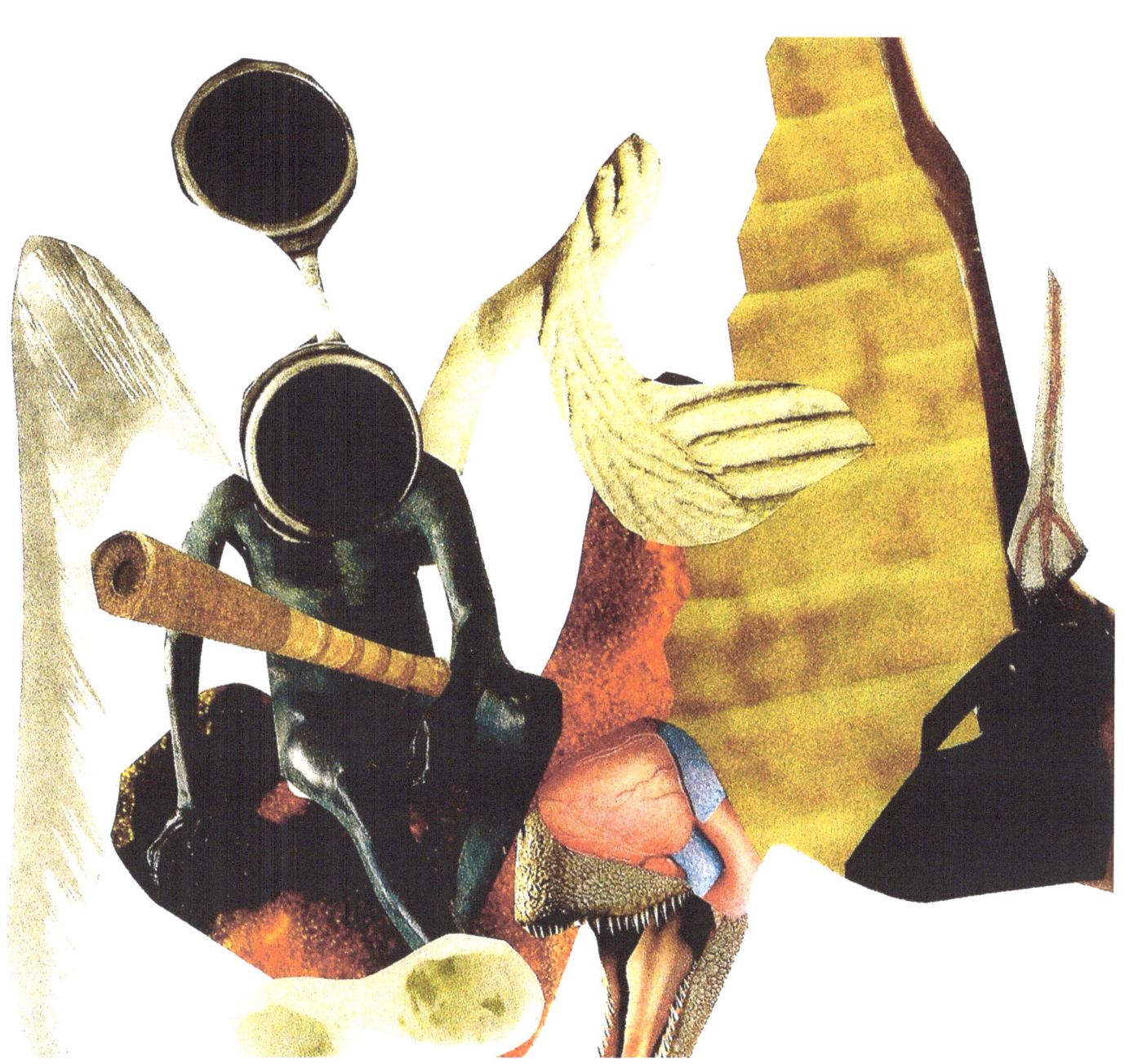

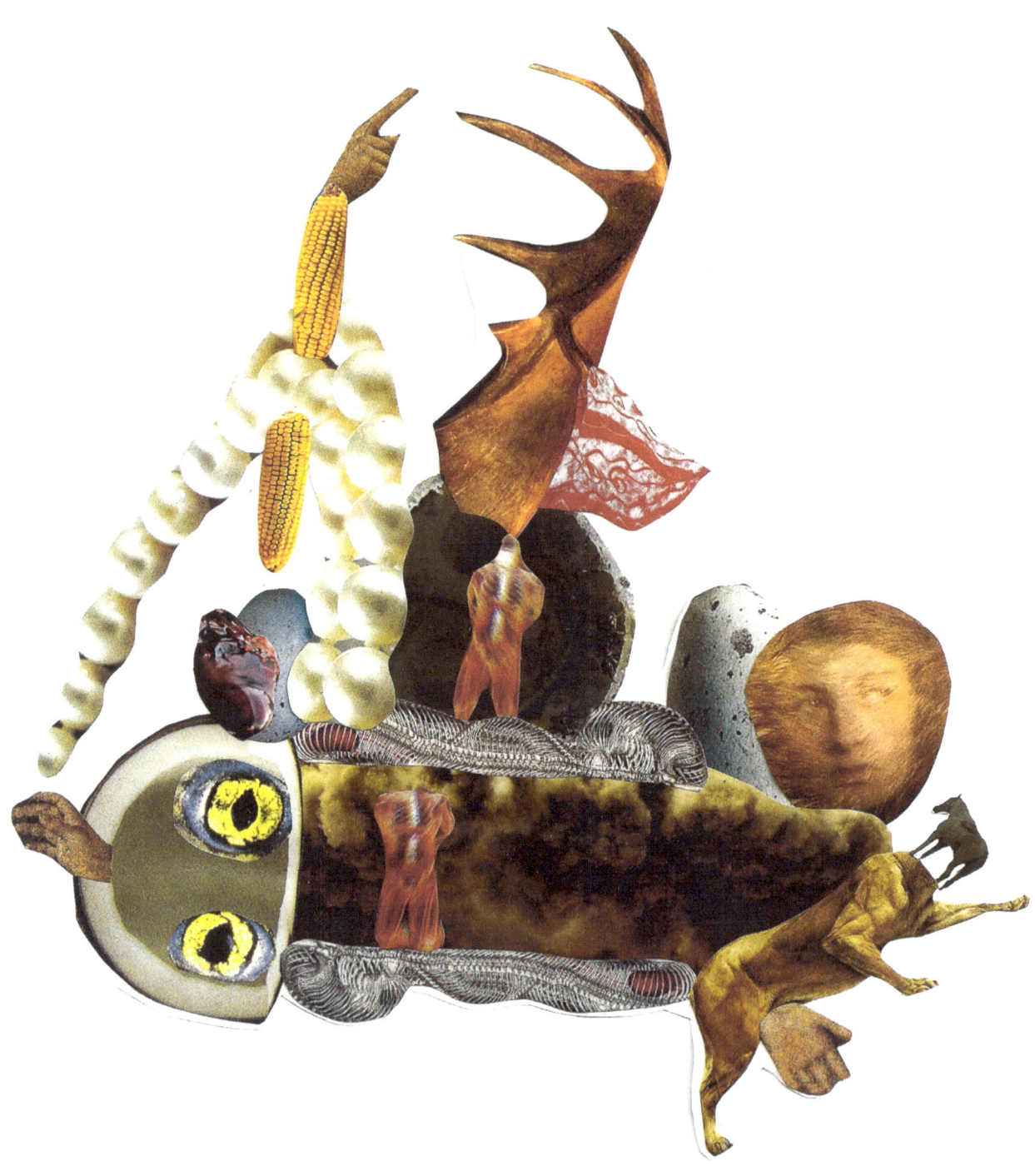

Prostrate As Fruition

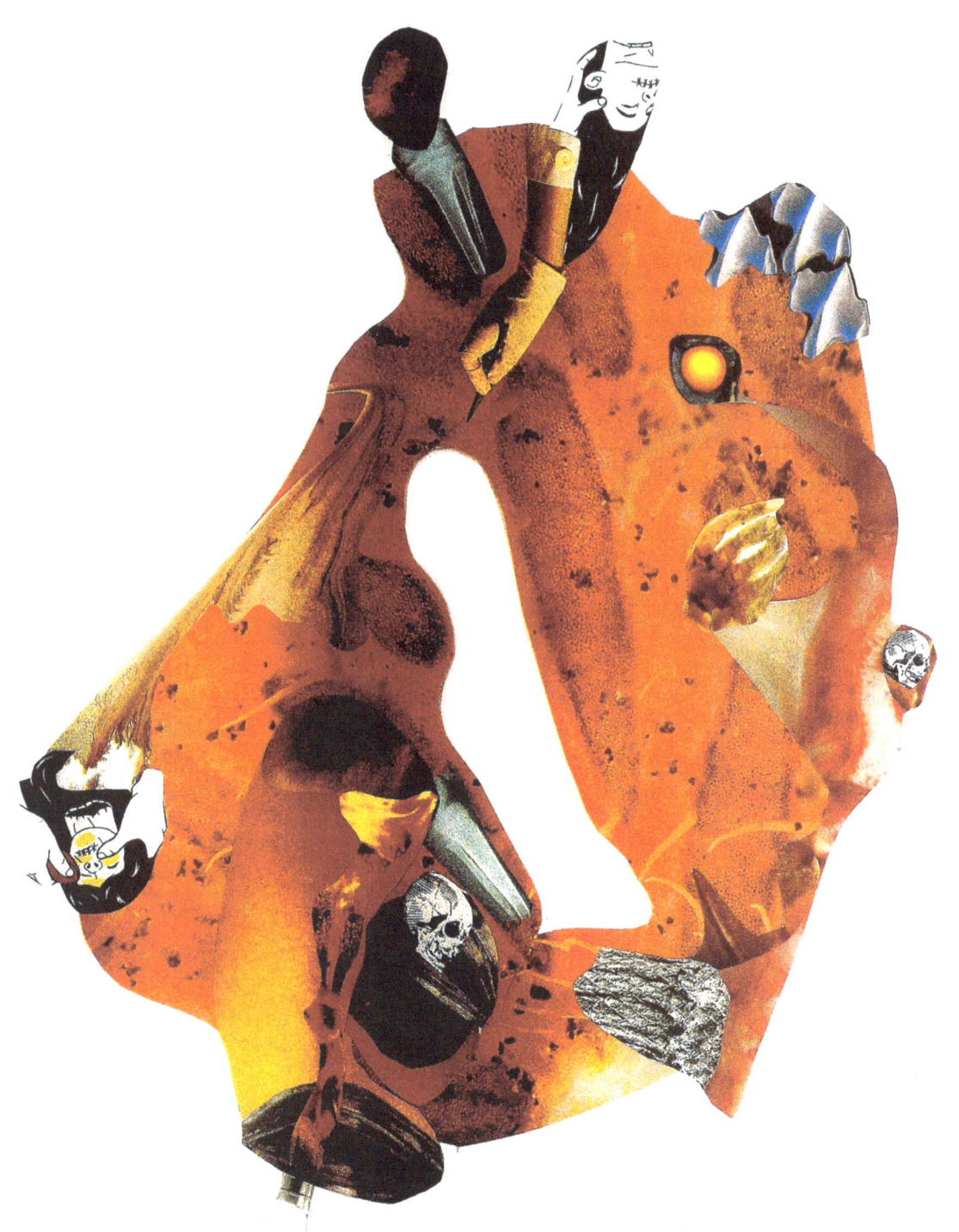

Put Pressure On The Eyes With The Thumb 63

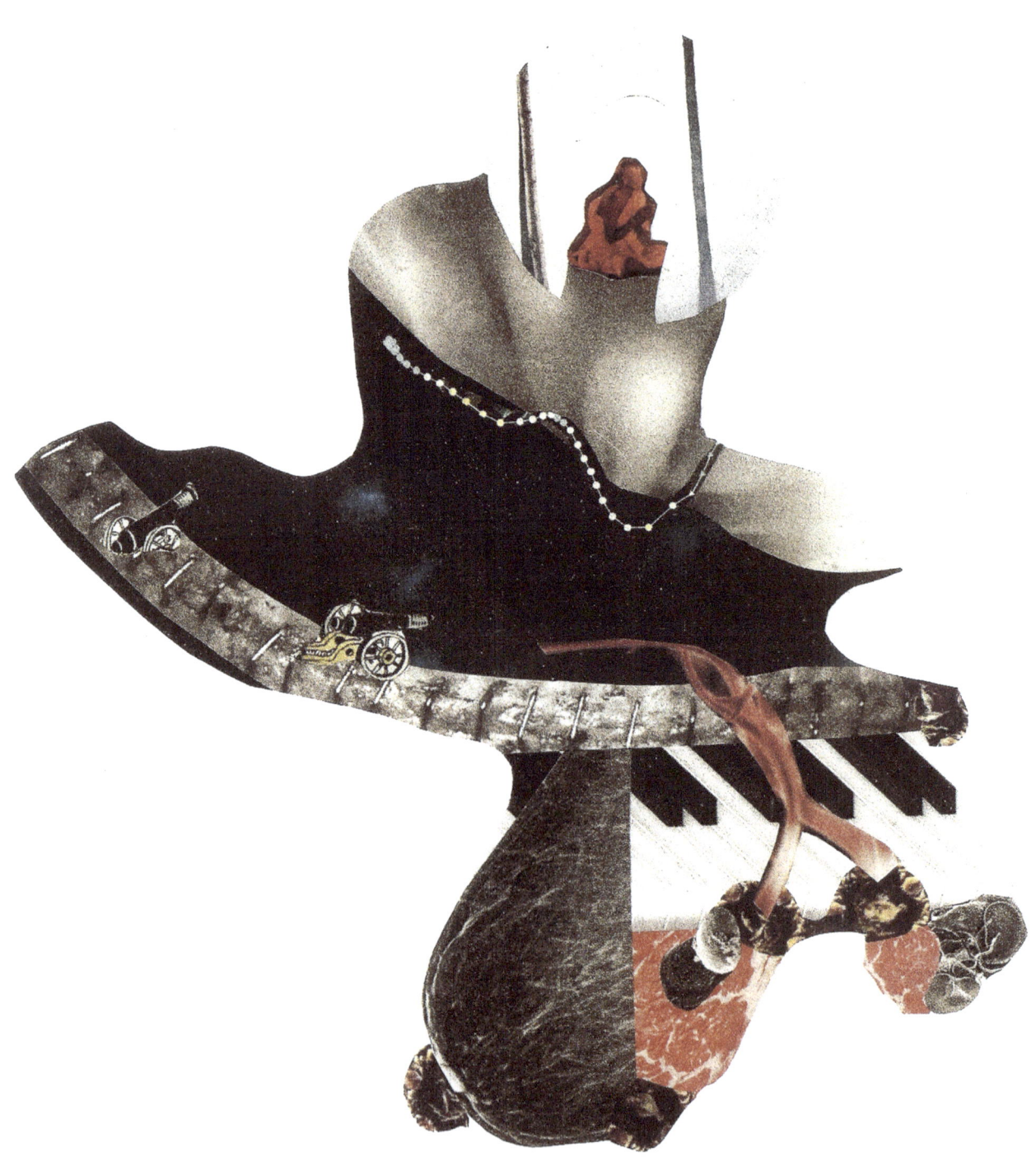

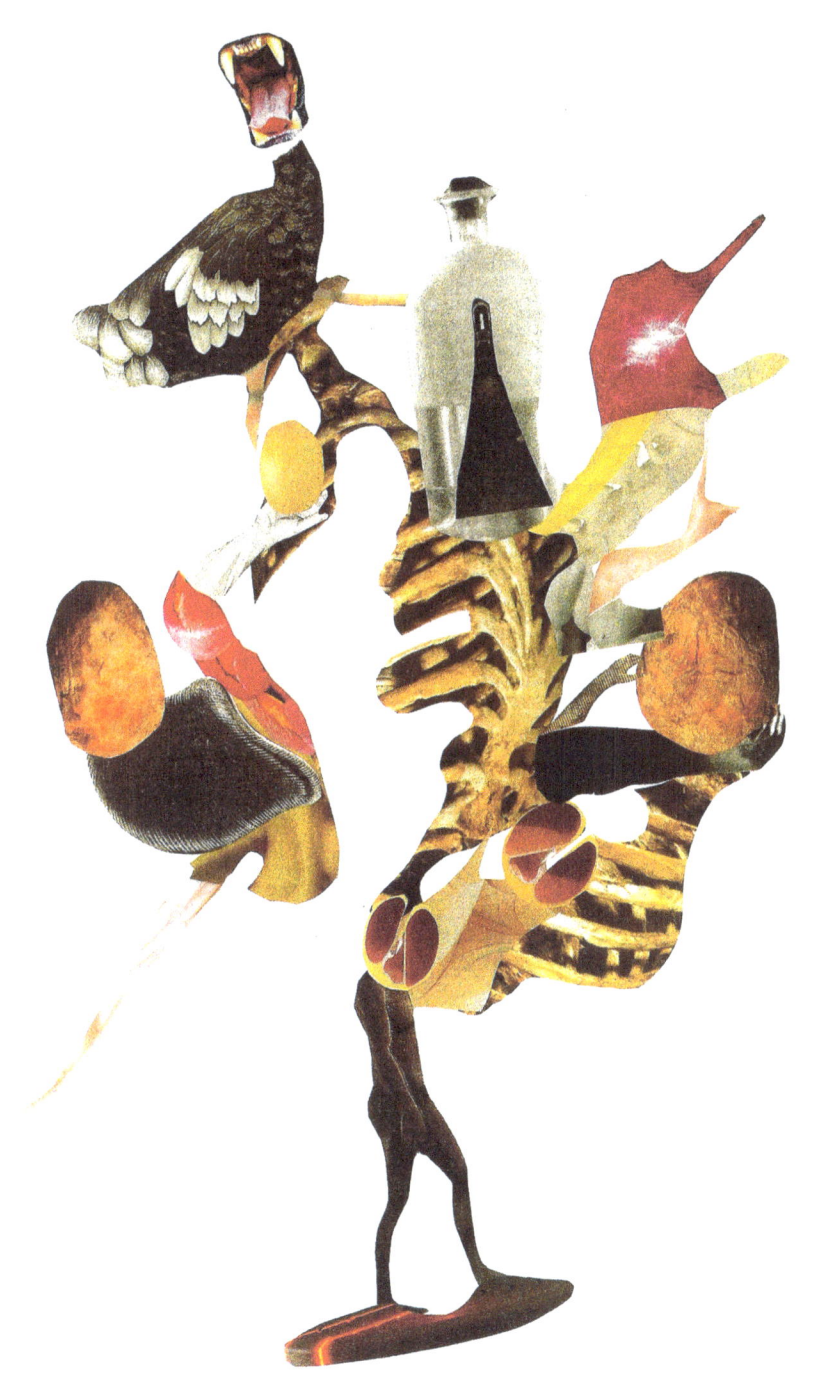

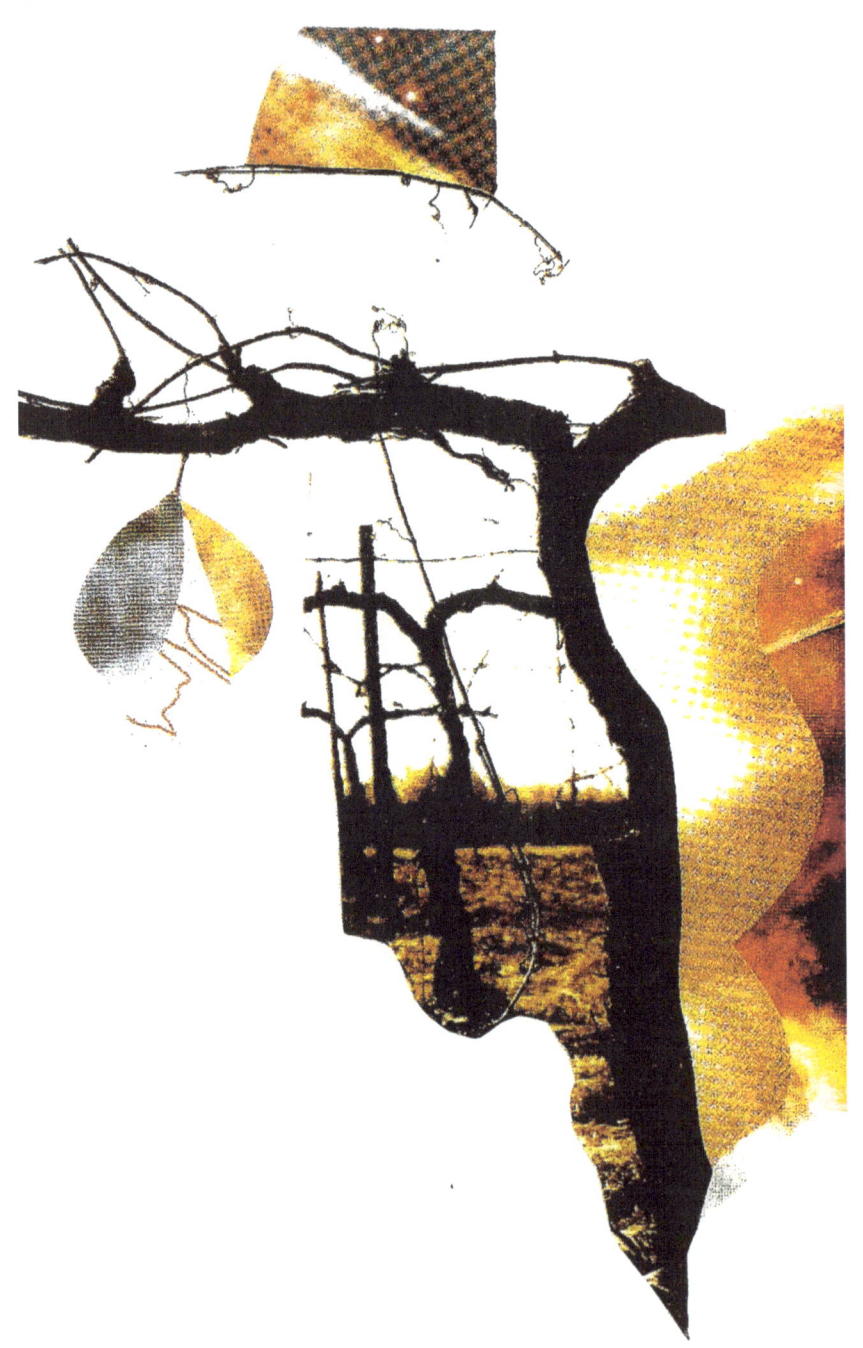

Effeminate Erection

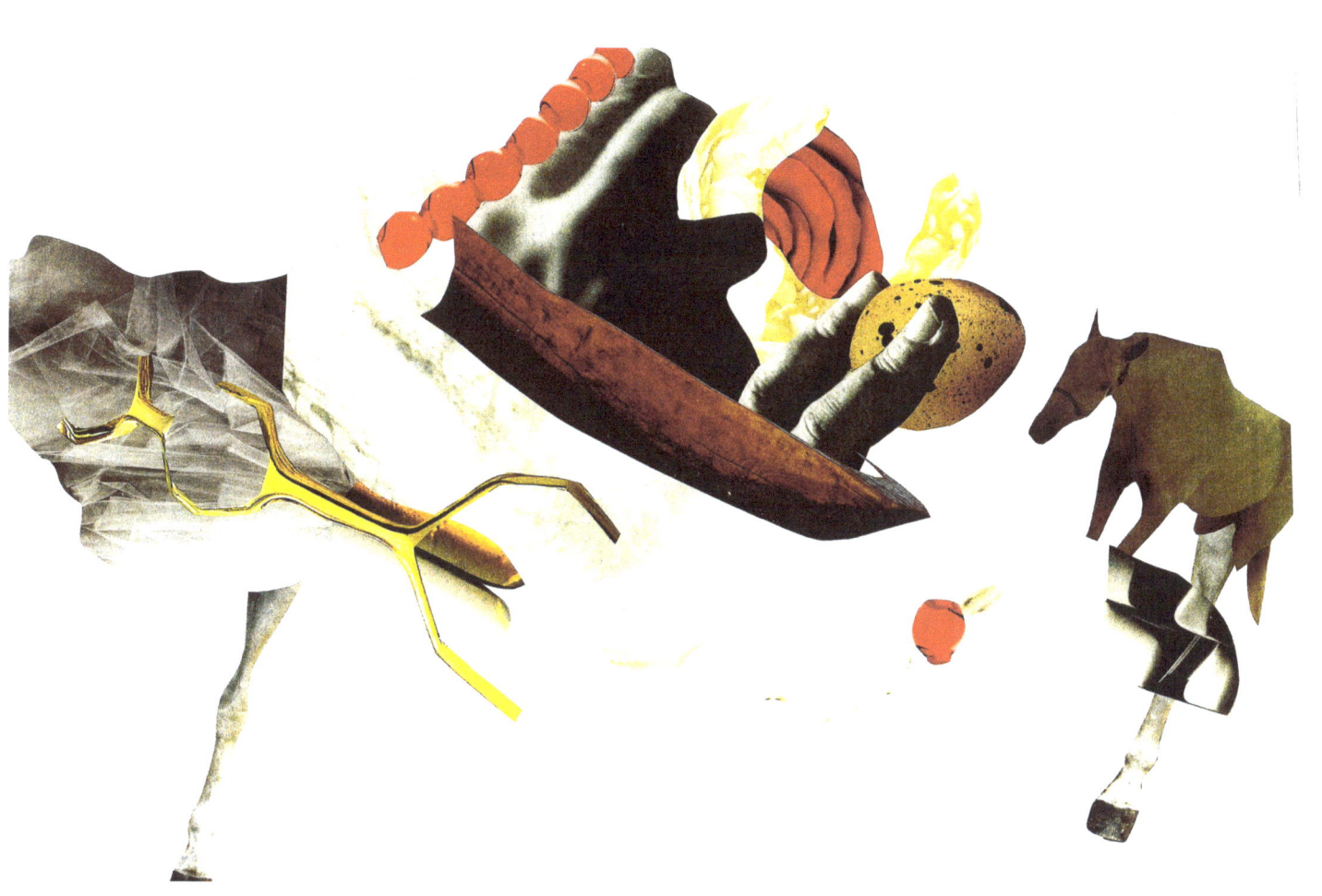

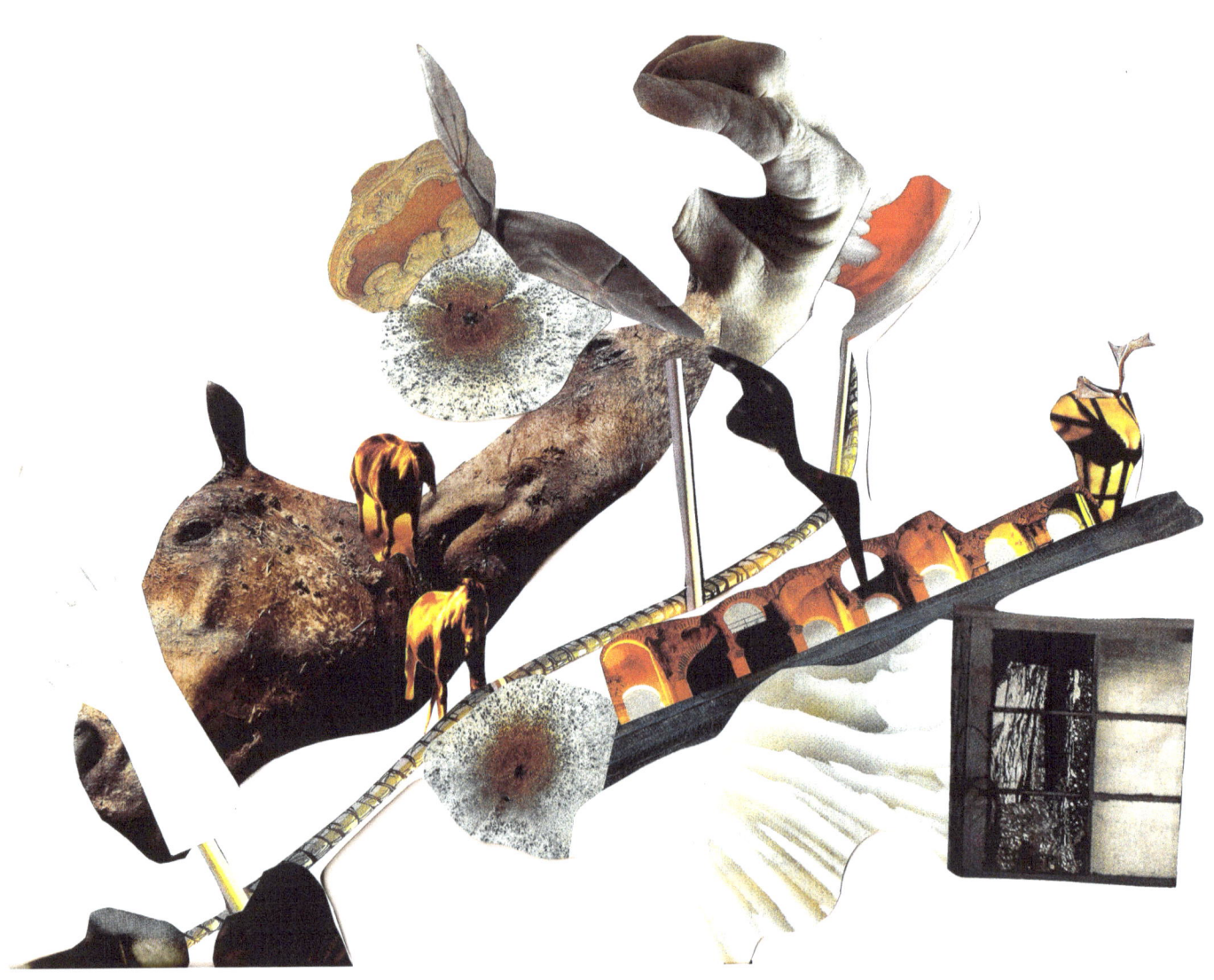

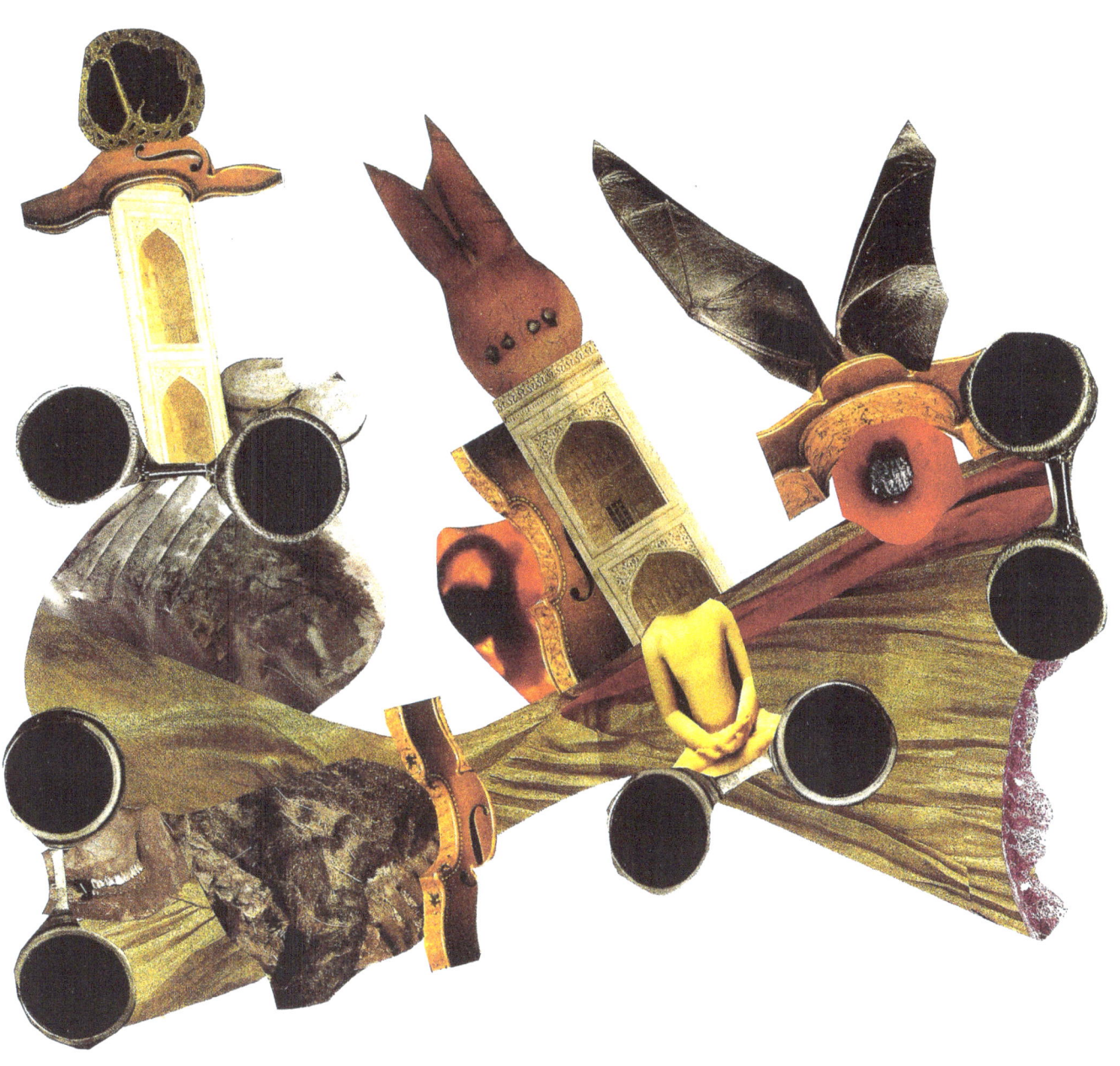

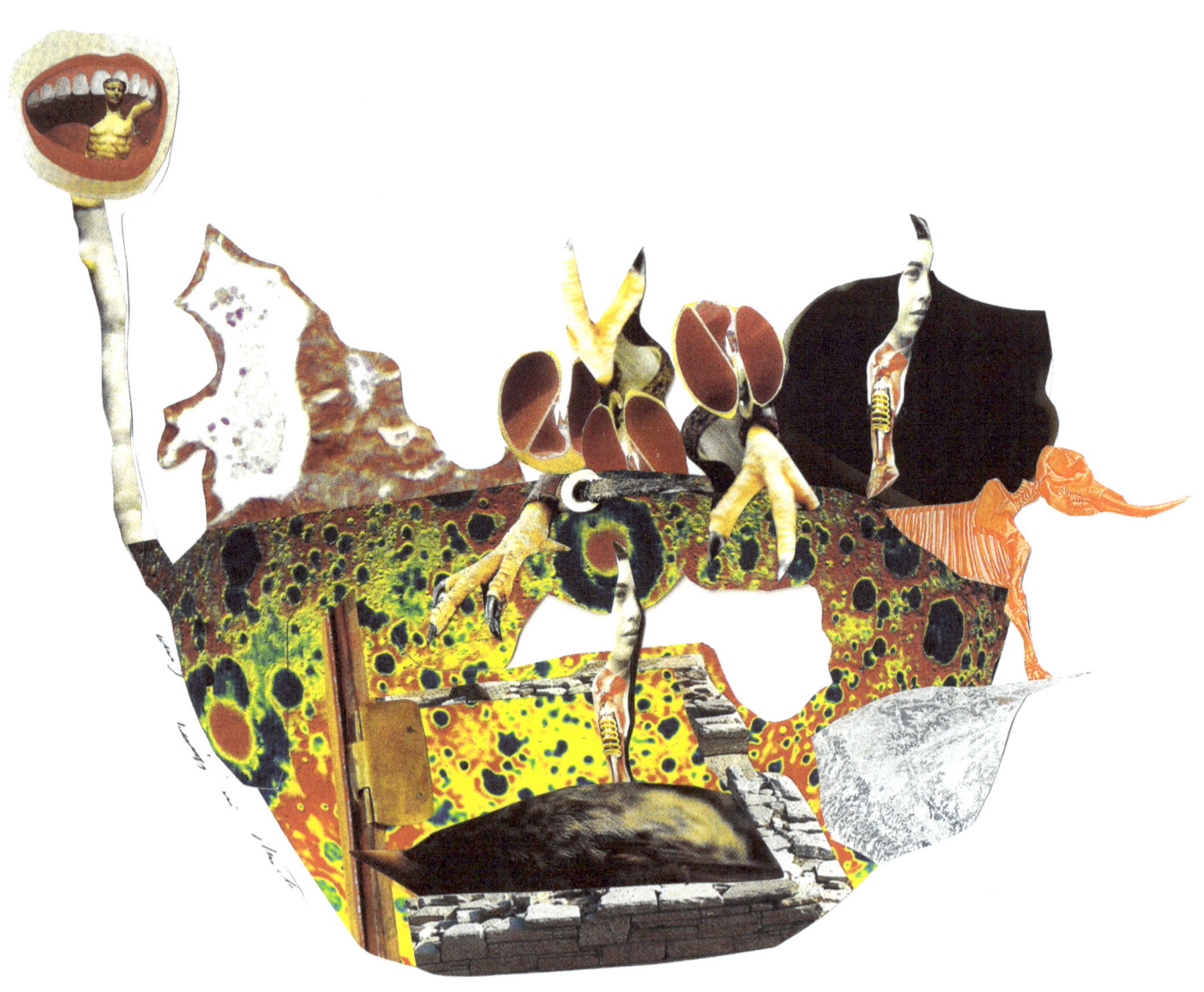

Slashed The Self-Portrait

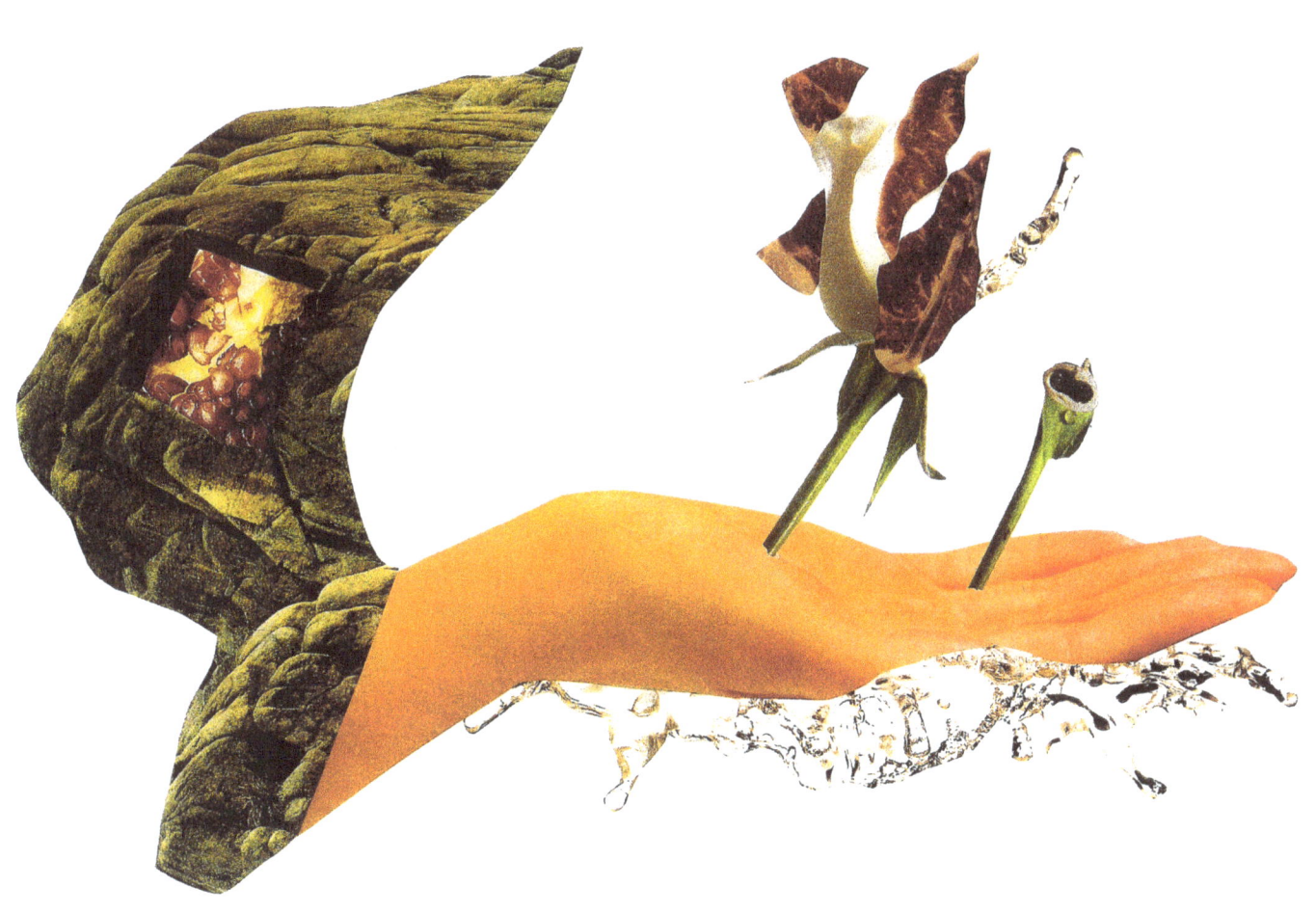

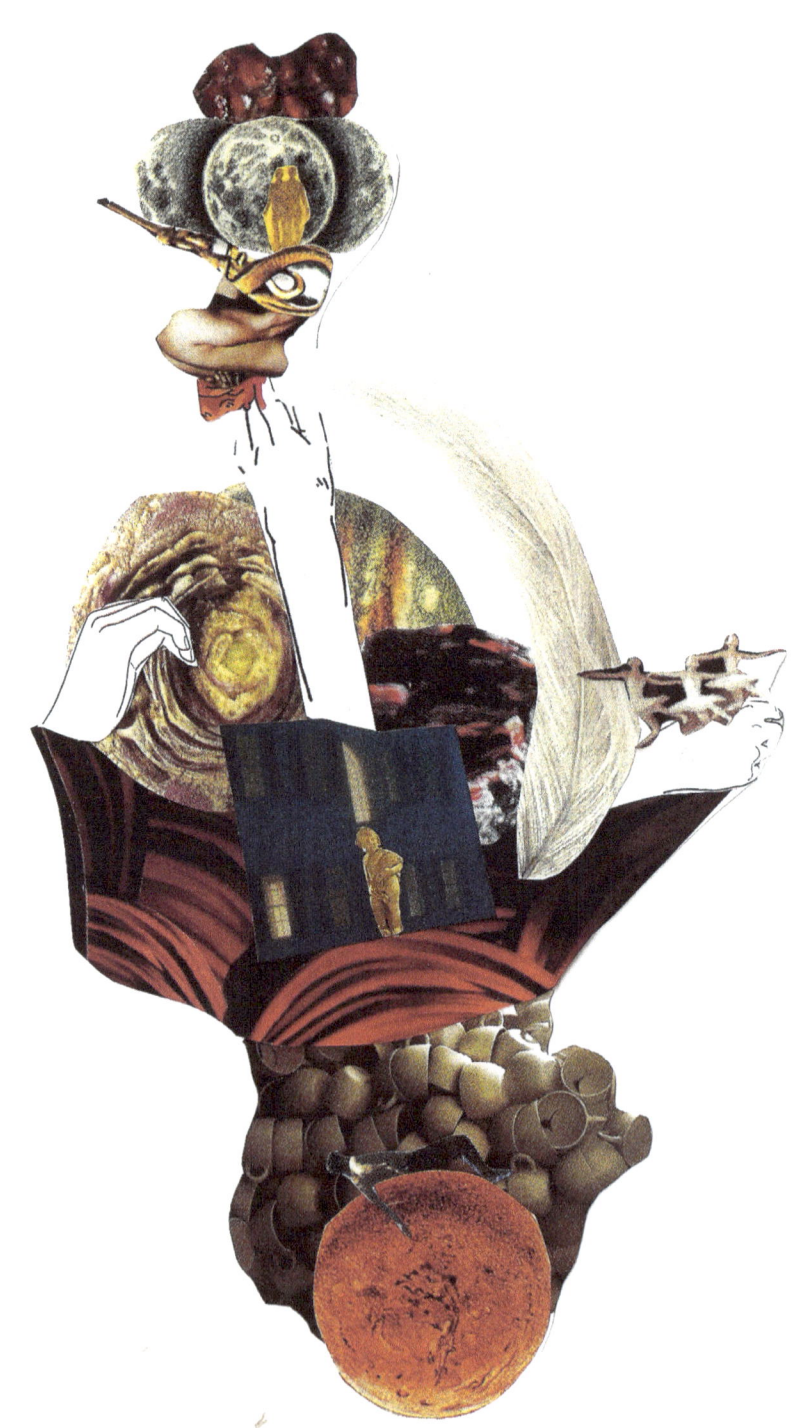

Self-Made Marriage Over Marred Inheritances

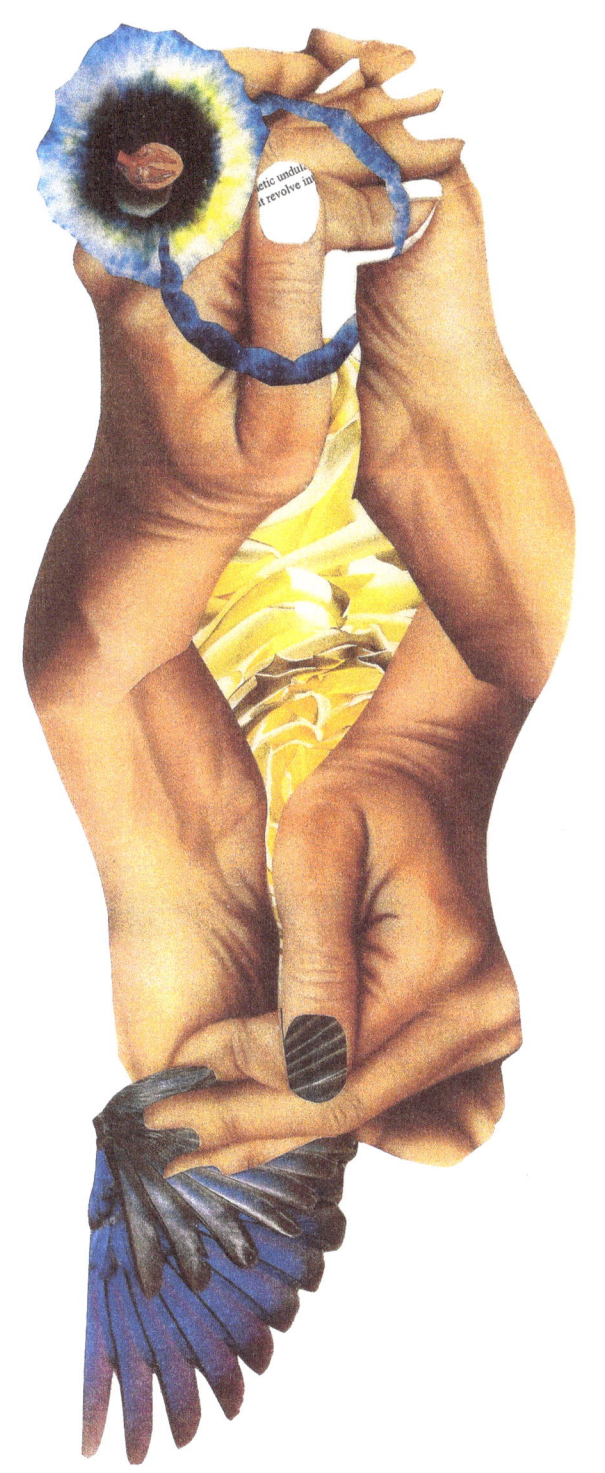

Asymptotic Lover

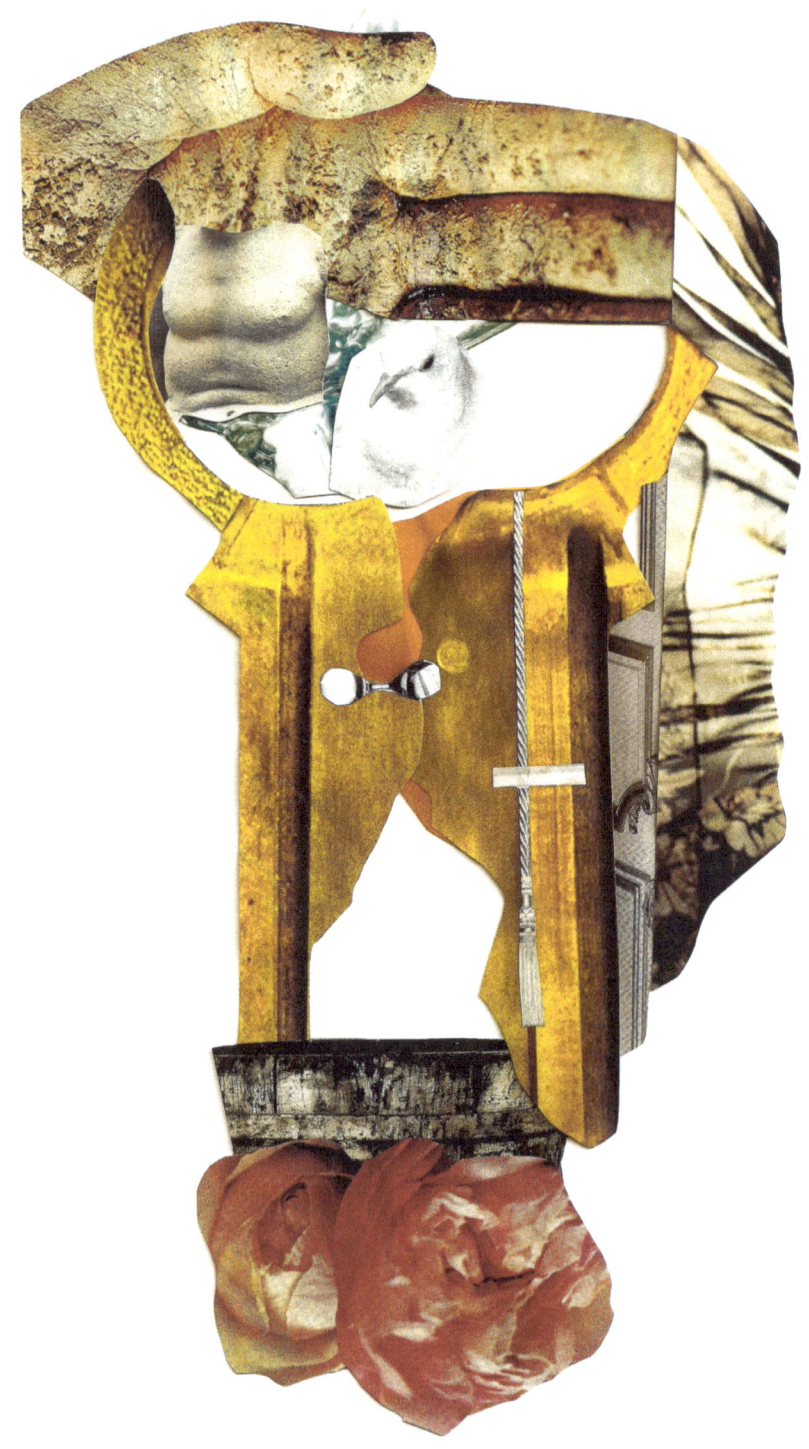

And Boi Has A Post-Binary Womb

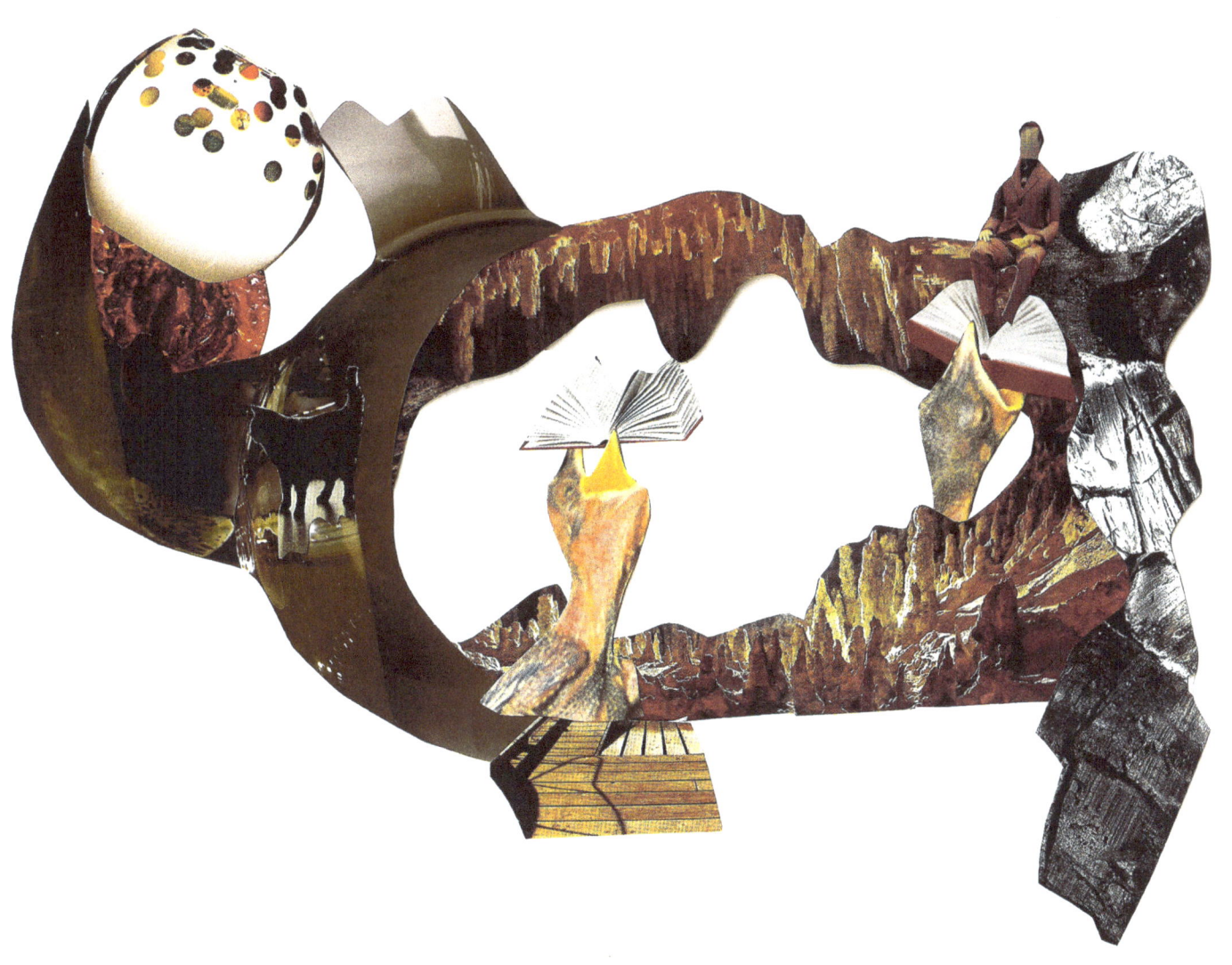

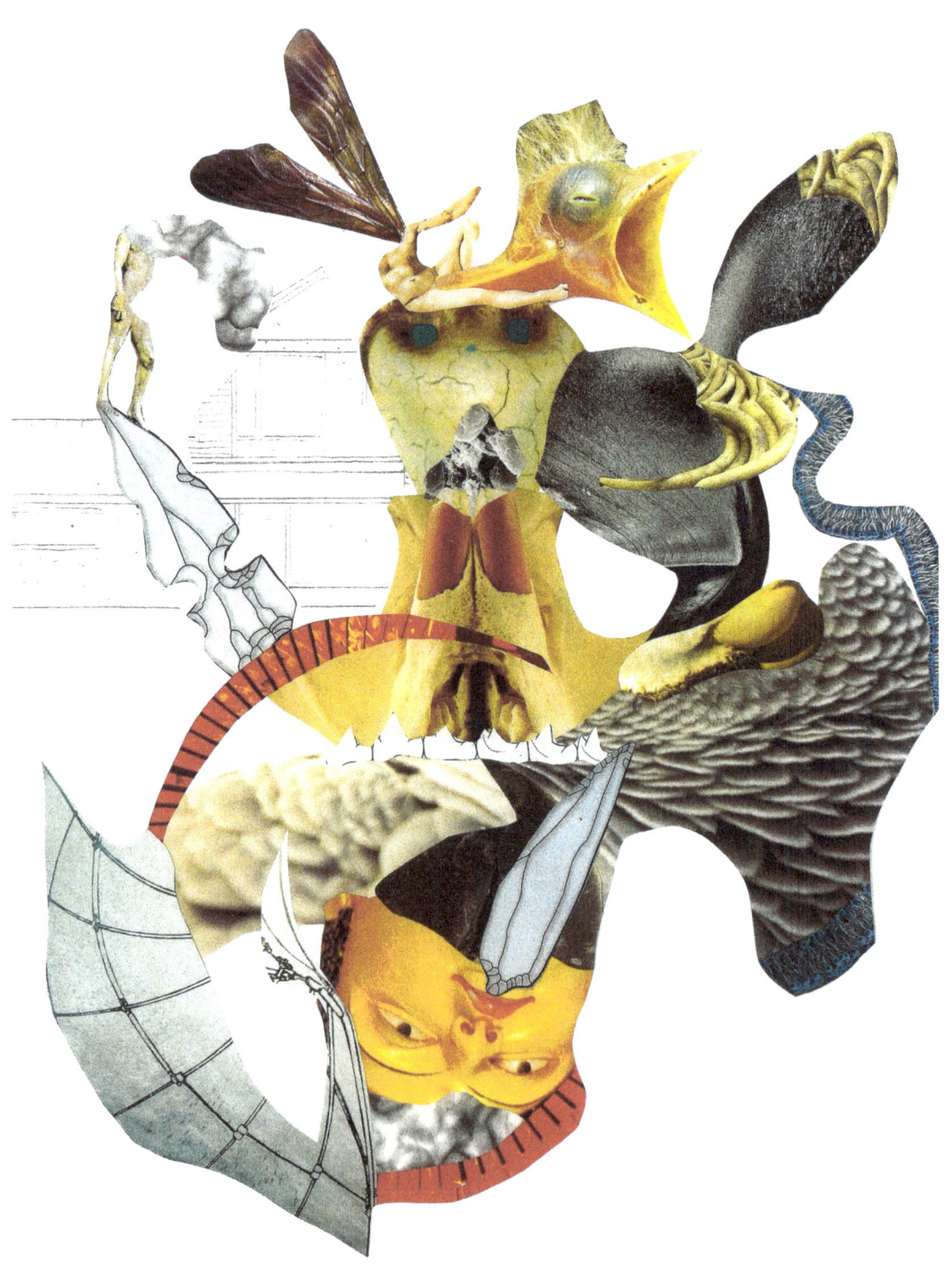

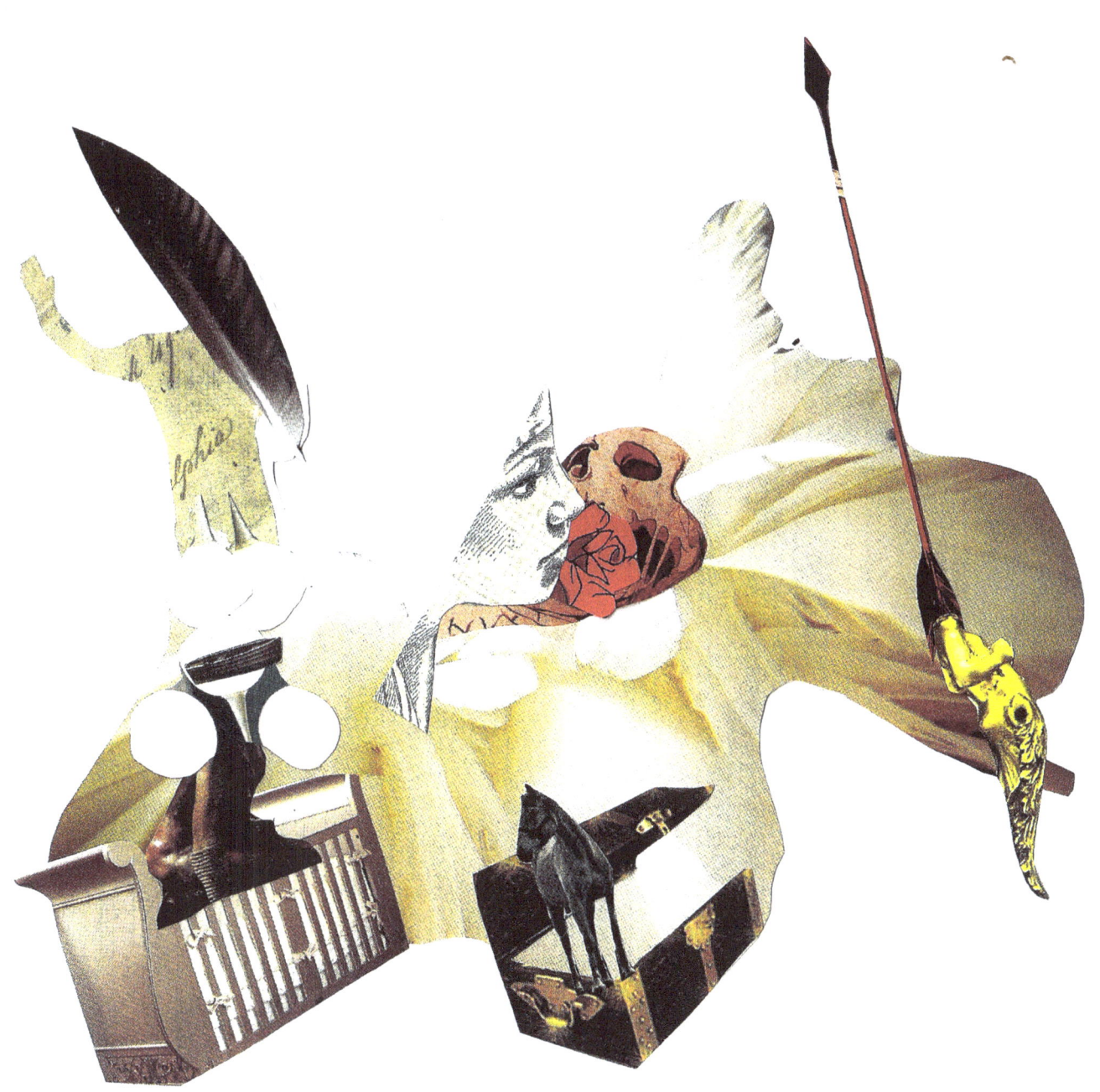

www.ingramcontent.com/pod-product-compliance
Lightning Source LLC
Chambersburg PA
CBHW050853180526
45159CB00007B/2661